Dialogue with the Rabbi
EXPLORING THE INNER PATH
OF LEADERSHIP

By

Paul F. Sincock

Trafford Publishing / www.trafford.com

I

The author welcome comments at: psincock@uswest.net

Printed in Canada

Canadian Cataloguing in Publication Data

Sincock, Paul F. (Paul French),
  Dialogue with the rabbi: Exploring the inner path of leadership

  ISBN 1-55212-324-2

  1. Self-realization. I. Title.
BF637.L4S56 2000   158.1   C99-911358-5

TRAFFORD

This book was published *on-demand* in cooperation with Trafford Publishing.
On-demand publishing is a unique process and service of making a book available for retail sale to the public taking advantage of on-demand manufacturing and Internet marketing.
On-demand publishing includes promotions, retail sales, manufacturing, order fulfilment, accounting and collecting royalties on behalf of the author.

Suite 6E, 2333 Government St., Victoria, B.C. V8T 4P4, CANADA
Phone   250-383-6864   Toll-free   1-888-232-4444 (Canada & US)
Fax   250-383-6804   E-mail   sales@trafford.com
Web site   www.trafford.com   TRAFFORD PUBLISHING IS A DIVISION OF TRAFFORD HOLDINGS LTD.
Trafford Catalogue #99-0074   www.trafford.com/robots/99-0074.html

10   9   8   7   6   5   4

Dedicated to:

My family,
Extended family,
Teachers of the way
and
Future generations

TABLE OF CONTENTS

PROLOGUE

Leadership is the subject of hundreds of books, articles, lectures and seminars. It is taught in the best schools and universities. It is practiced in varying degrees by millions of people in all walks of life, in businesses, governments, communities and families. Yet there is a tremendous void of knowledge when it comes to developing the *inner skills* required for effective, responsible leadership. The rate and magnitude of change that will take place over the next hundred years will require a transformation our spirit, our thinking and our relationships with each other.

I have had the privilege of a widely varied career and set of life experiences. From managing large organizations, to owning and operating my own businesses, to participating in community non-profits, to conducting hundreds of educational seminars, to being a locally elected official – all have confirmed the need to re-examine our underlying assumptions of who we are, where we are, and where we are going. These questions are both philosophical and pragmatic. They are ultimately questions of leadership.

For several years, I owned an Alternative Dispute Resolution business in Salt Lake City. What I discovered in hundreds of mediation and arbitration sessions, in the context of settling disputes, was that few people had the knowledge or skills to resolve their own inner state of conflict which was fueling the disputes in the first place. Business executives, lawyers, doctors, contractors, educators, steelworkers . . . virtually every walk of life had the same blind spot. It confirmed my experiences of others I worked with in business, neighborhoods, non-profits, and local government. People who welcome change, who have learned to resolve upsets in their life, are much more effective in dealing with others, more reality-centered, responsive and open to creative solutions. Those that have difficulty with resolution, who resist change and hold onto the past, have proportionately more difficulty with people and conflict situations.

The issue, however, is not conflict resolution, or management techniques, or methods of being more effective with others – though these are addressed in this book. The issues presented in this dialogue are directed at our underlying ways of thinking, our worldview, our cosmology and its meaning in our lives. Leadership involves the capacity to see and respond to our environment, in taking initiative and responsibility in one's life and relationships. Whether the context is business, community or family, these qualities are reflected in our behavior. Changing one's behavior is a result of new ways of thinking and interpreting the world around us. *That* is the focus of this book.

The setting for the dialogue is the largest possible context. I believe when we actually *see* the larger perspective, when we learn our common story and our shared journey, when we are provided the tools to resolve the daily restrictions of our life, a door opens to a new world of possibility. A long-term, sustainable future is our birthright as a planet. We humans are the most conscious of earth's creatures. We have the power, the dominion and the responsibility for shaping our common future. Whether we succeed or not, is an issue of *leadership*. Who will make the inner, spiritual changes required for that success? Who will assume leadership in shaping that common destiny?

The format is presented as a dialogue between two people. RABBI means *teacher* in Hebrew. It is a fitting name for the person of experience and wisdom. Rabbi is not meant to convey a religious perspective, but rather a perspective born of an ancient tradition. YOUTH represents all of us who are looking for answers in the world around us. Youth represents our inquiring nature, which is open to new ideas, open to change, and possibility. Youth is also a very recent and inexperienced species in terms of our planet's history, struggling with global issues never before faced. In Youth's hands is our collective future. ❑

Chapter

I.

CONTEXT

"Cosmology, though it is consonant with science, is not science. Cosmology is a wisdom tradition drawing upon not just science but religion and art and philosophy. Its principal aim is not the gathering of facts and theories but the transformation of the human.."

Brian Swimme
The Hidden Heart of the Cosmos

Chapter I.

CONTEXT

Rabbi How do you view your future?

Youth Well, I don't really know. I guess I'm worried.

Rabbi About what?

Youth About what I want to do with my life. I look at my friends' interest in the latest things to buy, fashions to wear, a job that pays the most money, the latest pop stars, or music or movie, or diet or drugs . . . their focus on the next party or good time . . . and I question why it bothers me?

Rabbi Well, why do you think it bothers you? The answer is in you, so think about it.

Youth I guess it seems so temporary, so short sighted. I mean it's like my friends just tune out the future because they, and I, don't feel we can make a difference. It seems like the world has been engaged in wars since the beginning of time and we still haven't learned anything. The cold war ended but the wars and violence continue. We're raping the earth of its resources and our leaders don't seem worried or even interested. We are preoccupied with corporate profits, the stock market, the latest political scandal . . . while people are dying of starvation and disease . . . even in our own country. I guess I don't want to be a part of that picture.

Rabbi   You don't have to.

Youth   What do you mean? What choice do I have?

Rabbi   You have many choices. It begins with your own thinking. Right now you only see a small part of the picture, the part you don't like. Your fears give power to that picture of reality and reinforce it.

Youth   But what other picture is there?

Rabbi   A much bigger and brighter picture than you can imagine.

Youth   What do you mean? I imagine many things . . . a better world, a more compassionate world, and more equitable world . . . but I don't see it taking shape anywhere. I guess that's what bothers me the most. That my dreams of the kind of world I want for myself and my family are just that . . . dreams. Dreams that have been shared by people everywhere, but they never become a reality. Maybe that's what worries me the most . . . the difference between my dreams and reality.

Rabbi   Your dreams are part of the reality. They are as real as the concrete you stand on. You don't yet recognize them for what they are.

Youth   What do you mean? Dreams aren't as real as the concrete! I don't understand what you're saying.

Rabbi   Here, look at this acorn. What do you see?

Youth   An acorn. I mean it has a hard shell and it's soft inside. It's a big seed.

Rabbi   What else is contained in the acorn? What happens when we plant it in the soil of the earth?

Youth   It begins to grow.

Rabbi   And if it has enough sunlight and water and nutrients and time, what will it become?

Youth   An oak tree.

Rabbi   So, is the oak tree in the acorn?

Youth   Well . . . in a way I guess it is. Otherwise, how could it become an oak tree?

Rabbi   So can we say that the oak tree exists as a *potential* in every acorn? Can we conclude that the potential oak tree is part of the structure of the acorn and determines what it will become?

Youth   I guess so. It certainly won't become an apple tree.

Rabbi   That's right. Do you think it possible that your dreams and aspirations are part of your structure as a human being? Do you think they are part of your potential . . . just as the mature tree is contained in its seed?

Youth   I don't know. I guess it's possible.

Rabbi   The dreams you described to me are universal. A better, more equitable, more compassionate world are contained in every society, every culture, every religion. Why do you think that is?

Youth   Because it's part of our potential? Could that be true?

Rabbi   Why not? Doesn't everything begin with our thoughts? If you want to build a table, don't you need an idea of the table beforehand? And from that picture in your mind, and the raw materials and tools available to you . . . you build the table. So the table actually existed before you built it, as a thought, an idea, a potential. All you did was transform it into a material reality through your actions, so you and others could see and feel and touch it. It became useful to many through your actions.

Youth   But that's not the same. Building a better world is not like building a table. It's not that simple.

Rabbi   I didn't say it was simple. But it's the same process.

Everything already exists as a potential within the universe. For example, the *way* to the moon has always existed, it simply took a long time for humans to gain the collective knowledge and experience to turn that potential into a reality that we could all participate in. But the *way* always existed. The way toward a better, more compassionate, equitable world already exists, otherwise it could never have been perceived as a dream of people from every culture and time. That world already exists as a *potential* within existence, but it will take those who see it and believe it, to transform that potential into a reality we can all participate in.

Youth   That's a big thought . . . and responsibility. I couldn't possibly do such a thing. I wouldn't know where to even start. It's scary.

Rabbi   I would also be scared if I thought it all depended on me. In a way it does, but not in the sense you are thinking.

Youth   What do you mean?

Rabbi   It's difficult to explain without discussing one's basic view of life, one's cosmology.

Youth   What does cosmology have to do with building a better world? I don't understand.

Rabbi   By cosmology I simply mean the basic story of the universe. Every people have a cosmology. It's really the primary structure of thought. Once a people figure that out, according to their experience and perceptions, then out of that they learn who they are and begin to shape their society, customs and institutions. The crisis that we are in today, which you are so concerned about, is because we are still operating out of an old cosmology, an old way of thinking, that is no longer functional. It's obsolete.

Youth   I still don't understand why our thinking is obsolete and how that creates a crisis. What do you mean?

Rabbi   I mean that the way we think determines what we see and do. If you think the earth is flat and the center of creation, from your perceptual observation of the earth, sun and stars, then that is what you tend to continue thinking and seeing. And everything in your life is based on that earth-centric reality; it's your paradigm. So long as you think that way, its very hard to listen to Copernicus tell you the sun is the center of the universe. There are implications in our present way of thinking, our cosmology, that underpin all of western civilization and those implications are causing tremendous disruption to our relationships and life support system. Our current western paradigm is so inadequate for what we are dealing with that we need to re-examine who we are, where we are going and what we must do to create outcomes we want. That's what I mean by obsolete . . . it doesn't work any more.

Youth   But if our thinking is obsolete and doesn't work any more, how can we change it from *inside* that thinking?

Rabbi   Good question. By first understanding our present
thinking, our current cosmology, and discovering why it no
longer works. For example, the native peoples that lived in
this part of our North American continent had a very different
cosmology than the people of European civilizations. It gives
a good example of how we see this leading to a whole set of
factors that influenced how those civilizations evolved.

Youth   You mean like the Hopi, Navaho, Mohicans and other
native tribes?

Rabbi   Yes. Native peoples, for instance, believed that the
Great Spirit lived inside the earth, that the earth was made up
of spirit, that if anything was, if it breathed and lived, it was
because they were participating in the breath of the Great
Spirit. So their stories enabled them to understand the nature
of the universe as eminently spiritual. The earth, therefore,
was to them a mother, was alive, was the womb - and
everything that came out of the womb was a relative. Now if
that was their basic paradigm, then it's logical that as they
evolved a religion and an ethic and a political system, it had to
make sense in relationship to their definition of the world.
Therefore, it could never have occurred to them to *own*
property, or to *buy* or *sell* parts of the earth, the *womb*. They
lived on this continent for the same period of time as
civilizations in Europe and Asia, but their relationship to the
earth was totally different. Their wisdom and their knowledge
and all that evolution of time did not enable them to develop
the material world. Rather, they spent their emphasis on

developing the inner person because they didn't regard the world as a *thing* . . . it would never have entered their minds.

Youth   Yes, that's very different than we think today.

Rabbi   When we look at the cosmology of the west, we begin to see how we created the structure of thought that has so characterized our evolution. There are three basic implications of our cosmology. First, every people have conceived of an organizing principle behind the material reality of the world. However we imagine that principle and by whatever name we assign to it, I call it God by the way, it was seen as being totally out of this world, transcendent, greater than, over the world, other than the world. The realm of that reality was non-material, in a higher place. Our cosmology holds the human as being related to that reality, but to achieve a relationship humans have to *transcend* the material world. Which led to a perception of the world as alien and apart from the non-material, isolated, not included. It left an impression of the world as a total material reality; a *stuff*, an *it*, a *thing*, a *place*. Ironically, it was that very perception which gave us a perspective that was detached from it and therefore free to probe it, and discover it, and break it apart, and rearrange it and in probing it to discover its physical structure and energies. The more we learned about those physical energies, the more we could apply them and the more we applied them, the more was revealed. The more we learned, the more we applied. It's the story of science and technology, from the wheel to the computer.

Youth   What is the second implication of our present way of thinking?

Rabbi   The second is that our cosmology separates the human from the non-human. We assume a radical discontinuity between these realities with all rights given to the human to exploit the non-human. The non-human is not recognized as having any rights. All basic realities and values are identified with the human, while the non-human attains its value only through its *use* by the human. This has brought about a devastating assault on the biosphere and geosphere by the human species, especially in the twentieth century. The result of this mode of thinking are global changes to the planet and life support system which we are just beginning to glimpse and understand. Global warming, for instance, is a fact that we are just beginning to see and accept. Its implications for our future are not yet understood, but intuitively we know that humans are both the cause and the answer . . . if we want to change.

Youth   That's part of why my friends and I feel so helpless about the future. So much is being exploited in the name of economic development, that I don't know what will be left. I have the sense of a great loss of something that I don't yet see or touch, but which is very real. It's disturbing.

Rabbi   Yes it is. But the sense of loss and concern about the future may also be the voice in you of that better world trying to be born. Have faith that you will find what you need. Do you want to continue?

Youth   Yes, please.

Rabbi   The third implication of our western cosmology is the emergence of global institutions which perpetuate it. There are four: the government, the church, educational institutions and the commercial-industrial corporation - the political, religious, intellectual and economic establishments. Each is intertwined in holding onto the current paradigm, which completely dominates our consciousness through a global communications network. We hardly know its there. It's a simple message of the emergent, global consumer society: *humans exist to work at jobs to earn money to buy stuff they think they need.* It's the primary message of TV, radio, print media and even the internet. Millions of such messages bombard our senses until we become numb to their effect on our consciousness. It's becoming the dominant *world faith*, whether you are German, British, Soviet, Chinese, Japanese or American. Thomas Berry, a passionist priest and eminent eco-thinker once observed, "So awesome is the devastation we are bringing about that we can only conclude that we are caught in a deep cultural pathology, a pathology that is sustained intellectually by the university, economically by the corporation, legally by the constitution, religiously by the church".

Youth   So what can I possibly do with all this? It's frankly so vast and depressing that it's hard to think about.

Rabbi   Yes it is . . . but necessary. Yet among the growing debris of our current, obsolete ways of thinking are the seeds of new possibilities, new beginnings. There are cycles of life and death for everything in existence. So far, we have talked only of the cycle of disintegration, which occurs whenever a life form or institution or idea no longer works. It dies. There is also a cycle of the birth of something new, something that is more elegant and responsive to the new realities, something which holds infinite hope for the future.

Youth   That's hard to believe when all I see is what you just described. What could replace it?

Rabbi   A new and much deeper understanding of reality. Modern science has revealed in the past fifty years a totally new view of how our universe is ordered. Our old 17th century mechanistic, hierarchical model of the universe, upon which most of our thinking and institutions have been patterned, is giving way to a much deeper understanding of how both *order* and *chaos* are integral constituents of reality. We have learned that no matter how deeply we look into the material world, from the sub-atomic level to the vastness of the cosmos, there is an orderliness, a differentiation, a connectedness, a uniqueness and indeed, an intelligence at every level of observation. There are no smudges. At the same time, quantum physics has revealed that underlying this material world is a dimension of unpredictability and relationships that change in response to the observer. The observed and the observer affect each other by their relationship. No longer can we view anything as separate from ourselves. Our observation is part of the process that brings forth the reality of what we are observing. In physics, fuzzy bundles of energy become particles only when observed. We are discovering that the universe is a participative structure in which we are essential to its coming forth. We evoke a potential that is *already present*. Our entire cosmology is changing.

Youth But what does it mean in terms of our present crisis?

Rabbi It means our old cosmology is totally obsolete and our thinking and institutions must change to reflect our new understanding of the universe and our place in it. Science is revealing and confirming what religious teachings have intimated for centuries – that the entire universe forms a single integral, living community in what Saint Thomas referred to as the "order of the universe." That there are dimensions of existence that we can only glimpse at our present stage, but in which we all participate. Yet here we are only beginning to deal with the implications of these new revelations, the new science and new cosmology that we are learning about, not through intuition as our native peoples did, but empirically, scientifically, in a way that we have been able to observe and document.

Youth But I live in the present world, the human world, and I don't see it impacted much by these new revelations.

Rabbi You're right. We are just beginning to deal with the implications of all this, yet we find ourselves living and working and learning and existing within institutions which are totally rooted in the old, and are nowhere near capable of the flexibility needed to make the adjustment that's required. This is part of the anguish and pain and difficulty of the times in which your life is unfolding. This is the time we are living in, and this is the Great Work of our time: to somehow bring about that transition of thinking even while we ourselves depend on institutions that we know can no longer function under the assumptions they are rooted in. How to do this in a non-violent way, how to do this in a transitional way that does not produce chaos, is a critical question for us. It's going to take the greatest depth of caring, energy and commitment.

Youth   But where do we start? How do we start?

Rabbi   It starts with you. If you want a world without war and violence, you must first deal with the war and violence in yourself. If you want to resolve conflict among others, resolve it first in yourself. If you want compassion in the world, work toward that end in your own life. That is how a new world emerges, one person at a time. That is how you build a new identity and a new world at the same time.

Youth   That sounds so easy to say, but hard to do. How do I eliminate conflict in my life? I doubt it's even possible – because I don't see it in others, I don't see it in the world. And what does my identity have to do with it? I'm having a hard time understanding where this is going!

Rabbi   I understand. Perhaps we should start at a different place . . . with our story.

Youth   What do you mean, our story?

Rabbi   Everyone has a story about their journey in life. We also have a collective story in which we all participate and which influences who we think we are and where we have come from. Its part of our personal story as well. Do you want to explore that story?

Youth   I'm not sure how it relates to what we have been discussing and my resulting confusion. But, OK let's see where our *story* brings us.

Rabbi   Let's take a look at some of the aspects of this new cosmology, just to put it into a perspective that I hope will be helpful to you. Our present understanding is that the universe goes back some 15 billion years from its beginning to the present, at least that's how we approximate it based on the signals still coming from that event. We now know that this universe is an unfolding process, it's a spatial reality, a time reality, an inner reality as well. And what our ancestors could never know, is that it's *still* unfolding, *still* evolving, *still* in process, *still* becoming. It's unfinished. We now know, since we've probed the nature of the sub-atomic world, that the universe is not just an external reality, but that it has an inner, non-material, psychic, intelligible reality. I'm not a scientist, but they tell me that the universe was hydrogen for about seven seconds and then helium emerged. That was the beginning of it's unfolding. Hydrogen and helium were totally present to each other, not only in their external connectedness of elements, but also in the inner, non-material reality that was an integral part of that emerging process. It's as though some deep inner reality was clothing itself in the energy and matter of the universe. Eventually, these elements combined into heavier and heavier elements and condensed into stars, planets, moons and galaxies beyond count.

Youth   So, compared to the universe as a whole, how old is the earth and our solar system?

Rabbi   Our sun and the earth emerged about five billion years ago and share the same basic elements. So we are rather young in terms of the cosmos, but are products of the same creative process. Over millions of years the elements of our planet began to condense together forming the body of the earth. The heavier elements descended to the core of the earth, the lighter elements to its surface, which cooled and solidified. Gases and magma were ejected to the surface; eventually an atmosphere formed and some gases condensed into liquid as we became a water planet. Gradually, over a long, long time the planet stabilized and the advent of life was at hand. The elements through which this process was unfolding began to form amino acids, which came together as protein and simple organisms.

Life is characterized by an *inner response* of a form to its environment. A rock does not move or respond on its own but only through external forces of nature. Life, on the other hand, responds *internally* to those external forces. This inner response demands energy to sustain, which requires the search for the *other* without which it cannot live. The dynamics of the life process were set in motion: our planet became alive. Life has become the most dominant aspect of planet earth: it transforms inert minerals and water into living tissue that responds, grows, and reproduces. It's hard to think this way, because we're inclined to think of the planet as an "it"; but the subject we are really talking about is the earth, not as an object, but as a subject. And in its process from the basic elements of creation to the emergence of life, it could be said that an interior reality more capable of expressing itself was gradually emerging.

Youth   That's an extraordinary story, one I've studied in school. But not the inner dimension you added. Yet it's hard to relate to how long that process really took

Rabbi   You're right. Perhaps if we could take the age of the earth, which is about five billion years, and compress it into the framework of one year, we can begin to grasp it in our minds. We would see that it would take about four months to have gone from gaseous matter, to a solid earth, to the formation of the atmosphere and seas, to the advent of life. From amino acids and simple proteins to the extraordinary complexity of the genetic coding that brought forth vegetation, creatures that could be mobile, creatures that began to develop organs of sight, and hearing, smell, mobility, reproduction, . . . that incredible unfolding of genetic design took another four and one half months. In these last three and one half months life has spread everywhere upon the earth; it developed increasingly complex nervous systems, capable of responding and adapting to an ever changing environment, until finally, in the last twenty-four hours, it brought forth an organism with a skeletal structure, a nervous system, a brain system so complex, so highly refined, that the earth now awakened not just to life and the capacity to feed itself and heal itself and regenerate itself and govern itself - but now had the capacity to reflect upon itself. That's who we are. The human is that being in whom the earth has finally awakened to consciousness. Or, even more deeply, the human is the being in whom the earth has finally become conscious of itself.

Youth Wow, that's an entirely new way of thinking about who we are, where we came from. . . . who *I am.*

Rabbi Yes it is. You and I are those beings in whom the earth is capable of thinking, of remembering, judging, perceiving, analyzing, choosing, acting . . . and of deciding. For in our deepest definition, you and I *are* the earth. It's the earth that is the subject and we who are its inventions, its expressions. I believe that the source of all this is God, but whether Jew or Christian, believer or not, it really doesn't matter in terms of the process. This kind of incredible order and design and process has come out of that infinite capacity for expression. But humans must, at this critical juncture of our story, begin to redefine ourselves. Our assumptions, which have come from an old way of thinking, are leading us into destruction of the very life support system of which we are a part. And it is often very good people, ethical, kind, moral, compassionate people who are, at the same time, causing its destruction. Not because they are evil, but because of ignorance. The basis of their understandings are no longer functional.

Youth   I guess ignorance is never an excuse, but it has consequences I never thought about. Why is our way of thinking causing such problems? I don't see the relationship of our thinking to our present crisis?

Rabbi   Let's look more closely at our human story and how our thinking emerged. When you begin to see that in this one-year timeframe, the human has just emerged in the past day, we're only 24 hours old. It gives you an evolutionary sense of time, you begin to realize how very new we are, how very young, how very primitive, how very experimental. And in fact, we may be an experiment that doesn't work. It's not guaranteed. Because the crucial thing about the human coming out of this process is that we're consciously aware. The rest of the universe is on a kind of internal guidance system, on automatic. But we're aware, we're free, we make choices, and it's yet to be seen if that is for the good or for the destruction of the earth. Are you following this?

Youth   Yes, please continue

Rabbi   If we were to take this last day that homo sapiens have been around, and compress that into 24 hours, then we would see that for most of that day we really don't remember, we don't have any memory of it. Twenty three and one half hours of the day, we don't even know about - that's the tribal age where we became conscious and where we began that incredibly laborious ascent into the shaping of symbols, abstract thought, the development of language, of tribal culture, traditions and agriculture. It's an extraordinary feat of the human. But we didn't really begin recording our histories about the great ancient civilizations until about a thirty minutes ago! It was here that we wrote our cosmologies, our stories. From that vantage point our story of the universe was formed and from this we created our cultures, our religions, our economics, our politics, our education, our health care. . . they are all based on the assumptions of a prior cosmology.

Youth But why is this story so important? I understand that wherever we are in time, our thinking is a product of a previous period and conception of the universe. But why is this time period, now, different? Why so important?

Rabbi Part of the reason why it's becoming so imperative to look at this, is because when we really start to see what is happening in this transition period of our history, it's that we are going into a *totally different* epoch. It's a radical shift, not just a small change in the history of the planet. The movement of life from the seas to the land is the order of magnitude of the changes that are happening now. For we are changing not simply the human, we are changing the chemistry of the planet, even the geological structure and functioning of the planet. We are disturbing the atmosphere, the hydrosphere and the geosphere all in a manner that is undoing the work of nature over some hundreds of millions, even billions of years. And the genetic strains that we have extinguished will never return.

What's happening is that we have acquired such awareness, such knowledge and mastery of the physical dimension and how its processes work that we are literally, at this stage, taking the earth off automatic, internal guidance and bringing it into conscious human guidance. That's what's really happening. The earth's self-knowledge, which is simply what the six billion of us who live along the rim of the earth know, is of such a magnitude that we are now consciously taking the planet's life support system off automatic, and that's why it's so key that we look at it seriously.

Youth   You mean humanity is causing global changes? It's not part of earth's natural internal, geologic processes?

Rabbi   We humans are impacting the earth's internal processes, the life process, the geologic process, in ways we do not yet understand. We don't understand the implications of what we are doing or the long-term unexpected consequences.

Youth   I never realized the problems or implications were so enormous. I'm not sure we're ready for something like this, are we?

Rabbi   I don't know . . . I hope so. Genetics is perhaps a good example of what I'm talking about. When you look at it as a whole, very often we see it as little, fragmented issues that are coming out, in biogenetic engineering here and gene splicing there. But basically what is happening is that the earth itself has come to a self-knowledge about its life processes and how it works. We've broken the code of life, DNA. We've gone inside the chromosomes. We know how the structure of genetic memory is connected. Our knowledge of that is such that we can now take it apart and rearrange it almost anyway we want. This is actually beginning to happen. So this enormous process by which the internal genetic coding and all living forms have emerged over billions of years, in a kind of finely tuned balancing act so that the genetic mistakes were dropped, they got kicked out . . . this underlying process is now threatened by us, the human species.

By the time we arrived on the evolutionary scene, most of the experimenting was done. We received an extraordinary community of living beings who had learned to adapt and survive. Now what we are about to do, is to make our own decisions about which ones we want to create and put into this finely tuned balancing act. So, of course, the question is are we, as a species, the six billion of us living on the surface of the earth, anywhere near the level of wisdom or the level of integrity or the level of maturity to be able to do this with the same kind of truthfulness that the process did without us? Have we, in terms of our capacity to control that knowledge, the wisdom to deal with what we know how to do? We may very well alter the capacity of the whole to sustain itself. If that interference causes genetic breakdown, or the breakdown of immune systems, then the only thing that will have changed this extraordinary, ancient planet is its own consciousness. Human consciousness will have done what the earth without us could not do - because the entire thing has been coded for life . . . to self-regulation, self-healing, self-nourishing, and self-governing. It's extraordinary.

Youth   I'm overwhelmed by it all. I need to think about everything we have discussed. I need some time to put it all together . . . at least some of it. Can we meet again next week? I'm sure I'll have more questions.

Rabbi   Of course, whenever you want. ❑

Chapter

II.

CHANGE

"To live in an evolutionary spirit means to engage with full ambition and without any reserve in the structure of the present, and yet to let go and flow into a new structure when the right time has come."

Erich Jantsch

Chapter II.

CHANGE

Rabbi　How have you been since we last talked?

Youth　I haven't slept much. I keep thinking about the implications of what you said, of how our way of thinking is doing us in, the level of ignorance in the world, the story of our planet and who we are in relation to the earth. It's exciting to learn a completely new view of the universe and our place in it, but it's also disturbing. I don't know where to start.

Rabbi　That's a very understandable and realistic response. Is there a particular part that you have questions about?

Youth　I don't know what to *do* about what I've learned.

Rabbi　Do nothing. You're not ready. For now, it's enough to simply see it, to study it, to appreciate the magnificence of our story . . . and to be disturbed by what you see in the world. The simple act of observing helps bring forth the reality of it all, both in you and others.

Youth How can my seeing it affect others?

Rabbi Because we are all connected. Are you familiar with the story of the 100th monkey?

Youth No.

Rabbi Well, it's a true story about how change occurred in a group of monkeys on the northern islands of Japan. Scientists began placing yams on the beach of an island populated by a large group of monkeys. They loved the sweetness of the yams but it took time to clean the sand from them before eating. One female monkey began washing the yams in the nearby salt water, which also added to the taste. Soon younger monkeys joined in the new behavior. But most ignored it. It took time, but slowly the new behavior spread to more and more of the group, until the 100th monkey so to speak, began to wash its yams. Suddenly, as though a critical mass had been reached, all the monkeys of the group spontaneously adopted the new behavior. Not only among this group, but scientists found the behavior adopted by groups of monkeys on adjoining islands at the same time.

Youth How can that be?

Rabbi Because somehow the consciousness of each member of the group is interconnected. Scientists call it *morphogenic resonance*, but by whatever name it's a reality in both the animal and human dimensions. Have you ever wondered how a flock of birds suddenly turns direction simultaneously? Or the instinctual communication between bees in a hive? Everything in existence is connected – we just don't fully understand it.

Youth   So, how does it work in people?

Rabbi   In much the same way. Everything in the universe, including human consciousness, is connected. We are just learning how those connections manifest, such as morphogenic fields that are responsible for species memory and group learning. When enough people adopt a new idea or focus on a common goal it generates a *field of intention* and possibility that help create the conditions by which others are influenced. Eventually, when enough people adopt the idea the field reaches a point, critical mass so to speak, at which it is *suddenly* much easier for the idea to spread and be adopted by a much wider population.

Youth   I think I read something about this in a science magazine last year. But I don't know why it's important?

Rabbi   Here is why. Consumer research some years ago discovered when only five percent of a population adopts a new idea or product, it becomes permanently *imbedded* in their consciousness. It has reached enough people to ensure its ongoingness in time. If the idea or product meets a need and continues to be adopted until it reaches twenty percent of the population, it becomes *unstoppable*. It will eventually affect and influence the entire population over time.

Youth   Can you give me an example of this?

Rabbi   Sure. Computers are a good example. For years computers remained in the domain of big corporations and governments for data processing. Then personal computers emerged in the mid-seventies. Apple Computer's initial units plus new word processing and spreadsheet software made the personal computer useful and acceptable to many. Sales took off until they reached a critical mass. IBM entered the market and legitimized the personal computer among conservative corporate types, further strengthening the market. Finally, the graphic user interface, developed by Xerox, refined and promoted by Apple, and broadly marketed by Microsoft, made computers easy to work with and thus accessible to millions of people. Our ways of thinking, our vocabulary, our perceptions, rates of change in our business, cultural and personal life . . . have been completely changed as a result of the personal computer. Now the Internet, made possible by the personal computer, is giving rise to a global information revolution accessible to tens of millions of people. It will further evolve and change the way we think – about ourselves, our institutions, our relationships, the marketing and access to new products, knowledge and ideas. It will change everything.

Youth   That's a good example, one I use every day. But, why is this process of change so important in the context of our present crisis?

Rabbi   The significance is that it only takes a small group of people to influence and eventually change everything. There is a lot of leverage built into the process of change . . . for good or evil. Margaret Mead's famous quote is an appropriate description of this reality, "Never doubt that a small group of thoughtful, committed people can change the world. Indeed, it is the only thing that ever has".

Youth   That gives me hope . . . but also fear.

Rabbi   Why is that?

Youth   Because the forces of greed and power have the same leverage. The established paradigm has incredible power and it seems impossible that anything will change it.

Rabbi   Very perceptive. But remember that the current cosmology is not working. All the power in the universe can't hold it together. Its disintegration is inevitable. It's only a matter of time. The issue is, will enough people adopt the new cosmology and make the changes in their conduct and consciousness that is required in time?

Youth   How much time do we have?

Rabbi   Just enough. No more, no less.

Youth   That's not very comforting. What changes in our conduct and consciousness are you referring to? Who will make those changes?

Rabbi   You will make the changes, you will live that future, you and coming generations will give form to that which already exists but is not yet present to the earth. You must become it and live it. Old established habits of thinking and behaving are hard to change. They will be replaced by those who are open to new ideas, who welcome change in their life, who thrive on the challenge of the new, those who see a new vision of life – and become it.

Youth   But what changes must be made? Where do I start? What must I do?

Rabbi   Recall our discussion last week? You asked the same question and I said it starts with you. You have already begun. The unfolding story of creation is the beginning. It now resides in your awareness and upon your heart. Hold it in your memory as a story to be lived and passed on to others. It will assist in changing the way you see and respond to the world around you. You have also learned that all things are connected and that what affects one part of the earth, affects it all. You have learned how change occurs and can be leveraged to support life. These are all necessary parts of the change process. The issue is applying that knowledge in your daily life.

Youth   But how? Where? What do you mean?

Rabbi   Last week you were concerned about the level of violence you saw in the world; the wars that never seem to end, the rape of the earth's resources. Do you recall?

Youth   Yes.

Rabbi   Those are the *outer effects* of the way we think, of a profound ignorance. That ignorance, and the violence which is its outcome, is responsible for all the pain and suffering in the world. It's responsible for our assault on the non-human realms of existence as well.

Youth   Ignorance of what? The new cosmology?

Rabbi   Yes, ignorance of the interconnectedness and interdependency of everything in existence, everything that lives and everything that supports that life. Ignorance of our common cosmic story that you are just beginning to learn.

Youth   How does that generate violence?

Rabbi   First you will have to understand the nature of violence. How do you feel when I impose my will or my way on you without your consent?

Youth   I don't like it, I get mad, I resist it . . . I guess I feel violated.

Rabbi   And why do you feel violated?

Youth   Because I had no choice. It was imposed on me. It wasn't my decision.

Rabbi   Have you ever imposed your way on your friends?

Have you ever used sarcasm, threats, or intimidation to get your way?

Youth   Yeah, I guess I have. With my parents, friends and others. But that's not violence, is it?

Rabbi   Yes it is. You have discovered the nature of violence: *the imposing of your way or your will upon another without their consent.* We think of violence only in its physical expression, such as war, rape, killing, torture, bullying, assault, choking, pushing, shoving, etc.. But there is also mental and emotional violence such as criticizing, deception, belittling, lying, retribution, controlling, revenge, isolation, withdrawing, patronizing, intimidation, racism and prejudice, to name a few. Violence is also expressed on the spiritual dimension as a loss of hope, loss of identity, a loss of initiative; the belief that I can do nothing in the face of reality.

Youth   I didn't realize violence was all those things. I didn't think I used violence at all . . . but maybe it's part of how I relate to others. Maybe it's one of the tools I use to get my way.

Rabbi   Can violence ever resolve conflict?

Youth   Well, I guess it can. It brings an ending to the fight or conflict. Certainly that's what war does.

Rabbi   If violence resolved conflict, why haven't wars led to a peaceful world after thousands of years?

Youth   Good question ... I don't know.

Rabbi   The fact is that violence can *never* resolve conflict or disputes, because its nature is rooted in *power* and *control* over another. Why is violence increasing in our society and the world? Because we use violence to suppress diversity. The "war on drugs" or the "war on crime" are doomed to failure because the use of power and control create more and more resistance which actually empowers the opposite. Our adversarial legal system is based on imposing one party's way upon another. The outcome breeds anger and resentment which, taken collectively over time, help create the very conditions, crime and violence, which the legal and criminal justice must then "fight". It's an endless cycle of cause and effect that will never be resolved without moving to the use of consensual, non-violent, non-adversarial processes in resolving conflict.

Youth   This is new. I never thought in a million years, that I was part of that problem. It's sobering. But how can my use of those means be harmful, except to the person I'm dealing with?

Rabbi   Everything is connected. Our thoughts, our emotions, our actions spread out like ripples in a pond to affect others, just like the monkeys washing yams. By holding onto anger, hostility, resentment and other negative emotions, we actually help generate a negative field of energy that influences others. It gives access and consent for others to adopt those same negative behaviors. We pass it to our children by our example in holding on to resentment and hostility toward neighbors, friends and family. That's how violence grows in the world.

The imposing of our human demands upon the non-human dimension is also rooted in power and control, in violence. We do not see or appreciate that we are absolutely dependent on the biosystem and geosystem to sustain us. Humans have been plundering the resources of the earth and its species with devastating results. These actions stem from a profound ignorance that doesn't register that we are all part of a collective community of beings that are an *expression* of this planet. We have taken dominion over the earth, before we have gained dominion over our hearts and minds. We are still children in the garden, not yet fully mature, not yet ready to tend it with loving care.

Youth   How do we stop all this?

Rabbi   We don't stop it. We bring forth alternatives that work better. The obsolete will die of its own weight. E.F. Schumacher once suggested that we "ignore the dinosaur and focus on the gezzelle". In other words, don't resist the obsolete around you, focus your attention on the new responses to life which are emerging around us as we speak.

Youth   But how do we deal with all the violence and destruction in the face of this?

Rabbi   We start by understanding the underlying dynamics of conflict and change. We learn that all humans have the same basic needs, that conflict is necessary for survival, that conflict is an outcome of diversity, and how to transform the negative energy of anger and violence into a deeper understanding of who we are. But again, it starts with you.

Youth   That just went over my head. I don't understand how conflict is a necessary thing?

Rabbi   Let's start by examining our human needs. They are universal. No matter how you define yourself, as American, British, Chinese, Soviet, Christian, Arab, Jew, Muslim, white, black, brown, tall, short, fat, skinny . . . all human beings have the same basic needs, which is part of what defines our species and who we are collectively. These needs express themselves on four distinct levels or dimensions . . . the need for air, food, water, shelter, warmth, sleep express our *physical* needs. The need to understand our environment and our place in it expresses our *mental* needs. The need to love and be loved expresses our *emotional* needs. And the search for meaning, purpose and fulfillment express our *spiritual* needs.

These built-in needs define our innate *dependency* relationship with the earth, its environment and each other. We are intensely social creatures who have developed very complex civilizations, cultures, religions, institutions and a relatively short history containing part of the collective memory of our species. Throughout the emergence of human civilizations, a recurring theme has been responsible for the rise and fall of empires, peoples and individuals. That theme is the interplay of conflict and resolution, war and peace, destruction and renewal.

Youth   I still don't understand why conflict is built in?

Rabbi   It's part of the survival mechanism built into life. Would you agree that survival is the goal of all life?

Youth   I don't know. You would have to explain it to me.

Rabbi   Every living thing, from the simplest living organisms to humans, has a *will* to survive, to continue itself in time and space.   Survival is the deepest and most powerful instinctual drive in living systems.   It is responsible for the tenacious ability of a plant to push up through the tiniest rock crevice to the light; the ability of microbes to survive in the superheated cauldrons of geysers; the capacity of an injured animal to fight and struggle with a predator to the very last instant; or the unselfconscious heroism of a person risking his or her life to save a child from a burning building.

   The *will to survive* has a profound influence on how human behavior patterns emerge.   We are most familiar with survival at the physical level . . . the necessity of sustaining ourselves physically must be satisfied if we are to continue our existence.   This is the *prime directive* so to speak, since every other dimension of human life depends upon the physical.   But we also know that survival on the mental, emotional and spiritual dimensions also has its own necessities.   Here we are not talking about survival as the continuation of our physical existence, but rather a dimension of meaning.   The derivation of the word *survival* is "sur-vivre", meaning above life, or the highest life.   Literally it means to "live to the highest".   So when we talk about survival of human life, it must include the notion of living to our highest possibilities. Are you following this?

Youth   Yes. But my basic question has not yet been answered. Why is conflict built-in?

Rabbi   Be patient, it will come. We must first build a foundation. The next corollary is that *diversity is necessary for survival*. Diversity in living systems is necessary to adapt to a changing environment. You can't have a planet of just oak trees, or alfalfa, or reptiles . . . it wouldn't work. The natural life support system of planet earth *requires* millions and millions of species to adapt to changes in the environment, so that life *itself* survives. This is also true in the human dimension . . . we need a diversity of races, nations, religions, political systems, customs, traditions and cultures to survive. This immense diversity in the human dimension is a constant source of new possibility and adaptability to an ever-changing environment. It's actually a collective strength, not a problem as some people seem to think. Seen in the largest context, *differentness* is actually how we learn about ourselves.

Youth   How does that work? How do we learn about ourselves by our differences?

Rabbi   If all humans looked and functioned alike, we could have no sense of individuality because "I" could not discern that "you" are different from me; like bees in a hive who function from a collective consciousness rather than an individual awareness. I can only learn about who I am by noticing how I am *different* than you and others; shorter, taller, darker, faster, slower, smarter, quicker . . . are all terms relative to something else. In other words we are programmed to see the differences so that we develop a sense of our own identity. Thus, diversity is necessary for independent, autonomous human functioning. Diversity is not a *problem* to be solved . . . it's the truth about the way things are. For without the diversity of all life, we could never become truly human

Youth   That's a broader definition of diversity than I've heard before. Mostly, I hear about ethnic and racial diversity in the workplace, or bio-diversity in the natural world.

Rabbi   Yes, diversity is big because it's necessary for life. And now, here is why conflict is built-in: *conflict is an outcome of diversity*. Conflict arises in the natural world from competition for survival among species and individuals. This creates an *alertness* or *aliveness* in higher species, as between the hunter and the hunted, which helps life adapt and survive. In humans, conflict arises from much the same sources. Since humans have a dimension of consciousness that is far wider and deeper than other species, we have many more opportunities for diversity, and therefore, conflict to arise. Whenever "my way" meets "your way", and they are different, the potential for conflict and dispute is always present. To the extent that I insist on "my way", or am closed to "your way", conflict is a much more probable outcome of any relationship we are in.

Youth But sometimes its hard to communicate what I'm trying to say, or to hear your way. I often feel misunderstood.

Rabbi Yes, the very nature of communications leads to differences in perception that can lead to conflict. Consider a conversation in which I describe something to you. Your response is not exactly what I meant to convey; its meaning is *similar* but not identical. Thus, when you reply I see *differences* between what I meant to say and what you actually understood, or more accurately, what I thought I heard you say. Eventually, through successive approximations between what I verbalize and what you hear, we could understand each other completely, if that was the goal. Or, based on my state of being, I may feel misunderstood or not valued by you, which can lead to feeling alienated which can lead to conflict. Clear, coherent communication is not usually our objective. We *assume* we are communicating and we assume we understand what is being communicated to us. Often, neither is true. Thus, because of our *differences,* and because communicating is *inherently* difficult, and because of our individuation . . . conflict becomes virtually inevitable given enough time.

Youth So, if survival is the goal and diversity is necessary for survival, which leads to conflict . . . is that why you said that conflict is necessary for survival? Is that why it's built-in? Can that be true?

Rabbi Absolutely. This understanding of the built-in nature of conflict is significant because so many people avoid or deny conflict in their lives. When you begin accepting the notion that conflict is not a problem to be solved or avoided, but rather *a window of opportunity* to learn something about yourself and others, a door to new possibilities opens. When I sprain my ankle, I limit my mobility and seek medical attention. Pain is the signal that something is wrong with the body. When I experience conflict such as anger, hostility, envy, or jealousy, why don't I treat it the same? Why don't I see that conflict is to my *state of being* what pain is to my body?

Youth   I don't know, I've never thought of it that way.

Rabbi   The next building block to our understanding the nature of conflict and violence is this: *Violence is the attempt to limit diversity.* This is another way of saying differentness. Have you ever noticed how angry you get when someone is espousing a value system which is totally different than yours, say atheism? Or abortion? Or a different political philosophy? Why is that? Isn't there the sense of *threat* to your own values or ideas? Don't you feel like you want to *eliminate* the different opinion? Make it go away?

Youth   Yes, I do. It makes me mad and I have very little tolerance in listening to views I consider wrong or ignorant. Sometimes I get so angry I want to hit the other person, or totally withdraw from the situation because I don't know what to say.

Rabbi   In your *refusal* to accept what is *different* than your own values or ideas, lies the root of violence. The exercise of your will in denying the other and imposing your way . . . is the *act* of violence.

Youth   What bothers me in thinking about this, is how really pervasive the roots of violence are . . . in myself, my friends and others in our society. Again, it's hard to face the truth. We are exposed to violence on TV, in the movies, in pop music and videos. And not just physical violence, but sexual violence, emotional and mental violence. It's a pretty scary picture of our society.

Rabbi   Yes, sadly it is. Our American culture is one of the most violent on earth. We are encouraging other countries to follow our example in the name of Democracy and Consumerism, where our highest values are expressed in economic terms, like the GNP. We represent only five percent of the earth's population but consume thirty percent of its resources – *that* is violence. We frankly don't think deeply about the consequences of our thoughts, actions or way of life. We refuse to accept that by *holding onto* and *reserving the right* to use violence in all its forms, we are actually enabling its continuation in the world. We are giving energy to the "field of intention which shapes behavior" - only this time it shapes a world of violence and disintegration. The *only* place you can begin to change this reality is in yourself. There is quite simply, no other way.

Youth   So how do I deal with conflict in myself? Where do I start? What do I do?

Rabbi   Where does conflict reside?

Youth   I don't know, I never thought about it. I guess when I'm angry it resides in me.

Rabbi   Right. It resides only within a *person.* It does not exist "out there"; it has a reality only within a living being. Conflict is an *internal* response arising from one's expectations or interests, needs, values, or beliefs not being met, or being infringed upon by others, or being different from those of others. Therefore, the only person who can deal with *your* conflict is you! You are the only one who can *resolve* your own state of being. It *never* depends on the other person. Thus, you are always responsible for your own state of being. Blaming others or shifting the responsibility away from oneself only prolongs the conflict and escalates disputes with others. At the deepest level, you are *always responsible* for resolving all conflicts and disputes in which you find yourself. Therefore, you can blame no one.

Youth   That's pretty intimidating. But *why* do I get angry? Where does the anger or conflict come from in me?

Rabbi   You have asked a central question. *Conflict is the refusal to accept reality.* Conflicts, which manifest as anger, resentment, hostility, frustration, i.e. negative emotion, arise from our *refusal* to accept the way things actually are. They *blind* us from seeing clearly and responding appropriately in the moment. This is an important concept, so let's use an example. Have you ever become frustrated or angry when you are stuck in traffic and late for an appointment?

Youth Yes, many times.

Rabbi To understand the source of the anger, ask yourself "What am I refusing to accept here?"

Youth That I am stuck in traffic and late for my appointment.

Rabbi Does your *refusal* to accept your situation change anything?

Youth No, not really. I just get frustrated. It's a mild form of road rage I guess.

Rabbi Right. So you are *actually* late and there is *nothing* you can do about it. You are refusing, in that moment of anger, to accept the way things *actually* are . . . that you are stuck in traffic, which was *not* your expectation. You are *late* for an appointment, when you pride yourself on being punctual, which reflects on who you think you are. Is that right?

Youth Yes. It sounds so silly when you put it that way.

Rabbi So, your expectations of being there on time have been thwarted by *reality*. You are in a state of resistance and denial to that reality. Your anger does not change the situation, it only serves to alienate you from responding in a different way.

Youth   Yes, I can see your point.

Rabbi   In the Buddhist tradition, there is a meditation on the idea that, "everything is spilt milk". My anger over the spilt milk is my own refusal to accept that reality in the moment. *It has already occurred.* Nothing in my response can change that fact. The only choice I have is my *response* to what has already occurred. Viewed at a deeper level, one will eventually realize that *I can never make a first move* . . . I am always responding to something which has already happened.

Youth   What do you mean, never make a first move? How can that be? I initiate things all the time.

Rabbi   But only in response to something you have become aware of, something that has already occurred or is in existence. Even the artist draws inspiration for a new sculpture or painting or play from that which already exists. We are never first, but always second in the creation process.

Youth   So are you suggesting that I have no choice in my responses to everything that happens or is in existence?

Rabbi   Exactly. Your only choices are *acceptance* of what has already occurred, by responding or doing nothing; or *resistance* and *denial*, which creates frustration, anger and violence. Thus, I have no choice about the choices I have in any life situation. There are only two, *acceptance or resistance.*

Youth   You mean that's it? Those are our only choices in every situation?

Rabbi   Yes. The first choice of *acceptance* allows you the freedom to take further initiative in the situation, if appropriate. Your mind and emotional state of being are open to new possibilities and choices. The second choice of *resistance* freezes you in denial and conflict, restricting your consciousness and limiting your ability to respond appropriately in the moment. The outcomes of resistance are denial, conflict, anger and violence. The outcomes of acceptance are freedom, response, creativity and solutions. Which outcomes do you want in your life? The choice is yours.

Youth   I see your point. Obviously, *acceptance* . . . given the alternative.

Rabbi   From these examples you can also see that the source of conflict is ones self-orientation, egocentricity and ones unconscious expectation that things will tend to occur as *you expect them to.* Most of us are not *present* to reality as it unfolds in our lives. We have expectations about how things should be, we deny the reality of our own behaviors, we live in our ideas and opinions of others, as though our perceptions are *true.* When a situation presents itself that is *different* than our expectations, we object. "Oh, no", or "It can't be true" is often our immediate response. We resist, we deny, we get angry. In short, our perceptual experience of the world is largely created in our minds, which is what we become attached to. It becomes part of our identity, who we think we are . . . and the way we think the world is. So when reality confronts us with something different, we refuse to accept it.

Youth   Yes, I can see how it works. I must deny reality more than I realized, judging by my negative responses. How do I learn to respond differently, develop more acceptance of situations in my life?

Rabbi   When a person actually accepts a situation that is generating conflict, the conflict and negative emotion go away. By "accepting" I mean *surrendering to the way things actually are without objection*. It is an act of the *will* to release ones attachment. Usually this also involves a release of emotion or energy that has been tied up in "holding on" to the past or "my way". When this occurs, the person feels a new surge of energy and hope because all the energy previously used in resisting and fighting "reality" is now available for other use. *Responsiveness to change* is the primary characteristic of individuals who have learned how to accept reality and resolve their emotional upsets quickly.

Youth   Actually, I do know a few people who meet that description, are open to change, are always optimistic and full of life. But is resolving conflict just a matter of acceptance or giving in? It seems so simple, yet very hard at the same time.

Rabbi   There is a specific process you can use to resolve any conflict in your life. Perhaps we can explore that next week?

Youth   OK, see you then. ❑

Chapter

III.

PROCESS

" . . . I even have a superstition that has grown on me as the result of invisible hands coming all the time – namely, that if you do follow your bliss, you will put yourself on a kind of track that has been there all the while, waiting for you, and the life that you ought to be living is the one you are living. When you can see that, you begin to meet people who are in the field of your bliss, and they open the doors to you. I say, follow your bliss and don't be afraid, and doors will open where you didn't know they were going to be."

Joseph Campbell

Chapter III.

PROCESS

Youth   You're causing me big problems!

Rabbi   How is that?

Youth   First, I'm losing sleep, as I said last week. Same this week. Second, when I try to explain some of the ideas and concepts to my friends, I'm not very coherent and they ask questions I can't answer. It's frustrating. Next, as I observe the world around me on a daily basis, you know, my friends, where I work, the daily news . . . I see everything in a new way, a disturbing way, which leaves me apprehensive.

Rabbi   What is so disturbing?

Youth   I don't know how to put it. It's a feeling. A sense that people are going about their lives asleep, like they don't question what is going on around them, just living their daily and weekly routines, like hamsters in an invisible cage. They listen to the daily news but don't hear the underlying themes of consumerism, ignorance, violence, money, sex. Maybe I'm just tuning into all this for the first time myself. Maybe it's my own ignorance I'm confronting. I don't know.

Rabbi You're disillusioned. Welcome it, embrace it, love it. For you are becoming *disassociated* from your *illusions* about who you are and how the world actually is. You are becoming more reality-centered. Yes, at this stage of your understanding, it's hard to see much hope. You are between two worlds: the world of the old, obsolete paradigm we live our daily lives within, and a new emerging world of possibility which is slowly taking form in our midst. But have faith, your needs will be met.

Youth I guess you're right. The conflict we talked about last week? That's what I am feeling. I can feel myself refusing to accept the reality I am now seeing in the world. How do I deal with that?

Rabbi Do you recall that we talked last week about conflict as a resistance or *objection* which arises within you as a response to something which has already occurred?

Youth Yes, I remember.

Rabbi Let's explore this further and see if it might help you sort things out. Conflict is characterized by many behavior patterns, from slight irritation to raging anger; from criticism of others to withdrawal to sarcasm to jealousy and many others. The *way* you express your inner state of conflict is based on the survival mechanism that *worked* as you were growing up. You chose a response which allowed you to survive the physical, mental or emotional environment you were in at the time. It was based on retaining and holding on to your identity, your ideas of who you thought you were, your ego. Eventually, these patterns of expression become habitual so that, as adults, we rarely think about them and very often don't even recognize we are in resistance and conflict in the moment.

Youth   Yes, I tend to withdraw and not confront difficult situations, at least not directly. I need time to sort things out.

Rabbi   It's because that pattern worked for you as a child in your family situation. I mentioned before that conflict is to our psyche what pain is to the body. Each is a signal that something is wrong or dysfunctional. Each limits our mobility and range of options. The way we deal with conflict and physical pain is quite different, however. When I experience pain in my shoulder or ear, I know that something is *wrong*. How do I know this? Because I know the *right* functioning of my shoulder or ear is when I have *no awareness* of them at all. The body is designed to function without our conscious awareness. It is the instrument through which we experience our existence and carry out our thoughts and intentions. By "we" I mean the organized consciousness which acts through the physical body; that part which accumulates experience and knowledge; the part which we come to recognize as "ourself". When we experience physical pain, it *captures* our attention, we become preoccupied with the pain and cannot focus our full attention on what we are doing.

Youth   That's a very interesting analogy. I know that when I broke my ankle a few years ago, it definitely captured my attention because it was hard to focus on anything else for a long time.

Rabbi   Exactly. When we experience conflict or resistance it *captures* our attention in the same way. We cannot function as intended. When you are functioning at your highest, there is no *awareness of yourself.*   You are interacting with what is the focus of your attention in such a way that you become *lost* in the experience. You become so intensely engaged in what interests you in that moment, that there is only the *experience* itself. These moments are not limited to "peak experiences" described by athletes and others. It is having the sense of participating in a larger process of interaction without self-awareness. It may happen at times with a friend, or a child, or planting a garden or watching a sunset paint brilliant colors across the evening sky.   You "merge" into the experience of the "other" so there is no sense of separation; you become one.

Youth   I had an incident like that, I think. I was helping to build a lodge in the mountains with a bunch of volunteers. We had to lift this incredible wood beam and move it about a hundred yards. It must have weighed 1,500 pounds. I recall us lined up on each side of the beam and lifting it as though it weighted nothing. It just levitated off the ground and we were there guiding it! We were all in unison, all in step, there was no effort at all. It was a feeling of oneness, just like you described.

Rabbi That's a good example, because it also illustrates how we can work together toward a common goal in total unison, without self-consciousness. When we function at our highest we are un-selfconscious. Anything that captures our attention or makes us self-conscious inhibits our capacities to respond to life. Yet why don't we treat anger, resentment, envy and other symptoms of conflict as we do physical pain? Why do we live with this dysfunction? The answers are many. We view anger as acceptable conduct, just as we accept violence in our lives. We *use* anger to get us motivated into action, to justify our negative behaviors and opinions. We use it to compensate and justify feelings of alienation from others. Negative emotions are so pervasive in our daily lives that we actually think they are "normal". Most important, we have never learned that we can actually deal with and *resolve* conflict within ourselves, rather than simply stuffing it away and ignoring its consequences.

Youth Yes, that's my pattern for dealing with conflict. I try to avoid it, or not deal with it. Eventually, the negative feelings go away, but I usually have residual resentment toward the other person.

Rabbi Because you have not resolved the situation or the relationship. You carry the resistance within you, to be resurrected when another, similar incident arises. You avoid the truth.

Dialogue with the Rabbi   **61**

Youth   What is the truth? How do I avoid it?

Rabbi   You avoid and deny the truth of the situation out of fear: fear of losing control, fear of facing the truth about yourself, fear of alienating the relationship, fear of the unknown. It's the ancient *fight or flight* dynamic of life. You don't yet have the tools or knowledge to face and resolve your negative emotions.

Remember, no matter what type of person you are, no matter your position or status in life . . . learning how to resolve conflict within yourself will teach you more about yourself and others than any other single discipline. Period. We are not talking about massive behavior change. We are talking about the singular, universal experience of conflict and learning a process by which it can be totally resolved within yourself. Do this one thing and the rest will be added.

Youth   What is that process to resolve conflict in myself? How does it work? What do I do?

Rabbi   Remember I said that conflict only resides in you, so you are the only one who can "resolve" it? That it *never* depends on the other person or situation changing first?

Youth   Yes, I remember.

Rabbi   Therefore, you always have the initiative and the responsibility for your attitude and inner state of being. In order to transform this negative energy into another state through the process of resolution, we must start with awareness of what we are experiencing. We will then proceed through five additional steps in the resolution process.

The first step is, *what emotion am I feeling?* We have to become aware of the emotion first. Now, for the purposes of our conversation, I will use the term "emotions" to refer to a range of *negative* responses, such as anger, fear, betrayal, jealousy, hatred, etc. I will use the term "feelings" to refer to *positive* responses, such as love, trust, admiration, etc. OK?

Youth　Yeah, that's how I think about them now.

Rabbi　Good, then we can understand each other better. Emotions are the sensation of *resisting* something we become aware of. We are putting on the brakes; we are saying "no". The range of emotions we experience varies from slight irritation, to criticism of others, to gossiping, to hostile remarks, controlling behavior, anger, rage and the aggressive imposition of our will on others through violence. They vary in intensity, but are all the same dynamic. These negative thoughts and emotions mold the body so we can see their effects in the tone of voice, facial expression or body language. First, let's concentrate on the most obvious emotions, like anger. More subtle ones will come later as we develop proficiency. Do you have an example of when you were angry with someone?

Youth　Yes, I blew up at a co-worker last month. He was supposed to take care of a matter for me and didn't.

Rabbi　OK, the next step is to ask, *what is the source of your emotion?* What circumstances generated your emotional response? Is it in the past or present? If in the past, how does the current situation remind you of the past event? If in the present, what similar situation does it remind you of? These questions are intended to pinpoint the source of your *objection*, which is what anger is. So, what was the source of your anger in this case?

Youth   Well, Bill was supposed to cover me during a break. I had to get my car from the garage and was gone for about an hour. When I got back, I caught hell from my boss for not being there. Bill, as it turned out, forgot our arrangement and my workstation was unattended.

Rabbi   So, in this case the incident was current. Besides anger, were there other emotions?

Youth   Yeah . . . I felt betrayed by him as well.

Rabbi   OK, the next step is to ask, *toward whom are the emotions directed?* In this case it is toward your co-worker, Bill. The question is, why did it evoke so much emotion from you, especially since it's not your pattern?

Youth   That's a good question. It was an unusual outburst from me. I'll have to think about it.

Rabbi   Good, we can come back to this point later. The next step is to ask yourself, *what am I refusing to accept?* This is the *key question*, after you have an awareness of the nature of the emotions. You already know the answer. It is a matter of making the answers *conscious* to your mind. Try to frame them like, "I am refusing to accept that . . . . . ." The answer should always be framed so that you are the one responsible. So how would you answer this question?

Youth Well, I guess I was refusing to accept that Bill had forgotten our agreement, that he actually didn't show up.

Rabbi And when your boss told you off, how did you react?

Youth I was embarrassed at first, then defensive – I blamed Bill, I tried to shift the blame from myself.

Rabbi So in that moment, you were also refusing to accept a reality . . . that you were responsible for being at your workstation, not Bill. You hadn't told your boss and you didn't remind Bill to be there, right?

Youth Yeah, I guess you are right.

Rabbi So the entire incident was your doing and your responsibility. That's also what you were refusing to accept, right? You had an expectation for how it *should be* and the actual reality was different.

Youth I see your point.

Rabbi Do you know why you blew up at Bill, why so much emotion?

Youth   Well, I felt betrayed . . . I guess I felt hurt by him.

Rabbi   He did not *hurt* you, he did nothing. That's an expression to blame the other for what you are experiencing, to shift responsibility. You experienced hurt because something else is unresolved in you. Where else have you felt betrayed?

Youth   What comes to my mind immediately . . . is my father. He used to promise to come to my ball games when I was a kid, but was always too busy. He always had excuses. It hurt. I wasn't important enough to him . . . that's how it felt.

Rabbi   Good, is there anything else which comes to mind?

Youth   I have a very short fuse when it comes to people keeping their promises, being late, not keeping commitments.

Rabbi   Do you think it could be related to your childhood experience of feeling disappointed and betrayed?

Youth   Yeah . . . maybe it is. Now that I think about it, I never understood why those behaviors bugged me so much. I feel awful whenever I'm late, or forget to keep a promise.

Rabbi   Forgetting is an excuse for not being responsible for your own commitments. You don't forget what's important. A promise not fulfilled by you is simply not that important to you. Like your father's, right?

Youth   That's hard to accept . . . that my behavior is like my fathers. But I see your point, I guess its true. Wow. Maybe that's also why I get so irritated at people being late?

Rabbi Exactly. You have been refusing to accept the reality about your father. You didn't feel he loved you enough to keep his promises. No child wants to accept that. When you totally surrender to it, embrace it, the emotions you are holding onto will surface and dissipate, you will see more implications.

Youth Yes, I can begin to see that. Just talking with you about it helps, just seeing it . . . I never thought about the connection or talked to anyone about it before. What do I do now?

Rabbi You are doing it, you are observing a reality you didn't want to face. Your observation and acceptance will allow you to see more, learn more about yourself.

Youth Yeah, I see what you mean. But what about my father? What about Bill?

Rabbi The next step in the resolution process is *remedy*. Eventually, when you have totally accepted the source of feeling betrayed by your father, and blaming Bill, you may want to talk to each of them. The conflict you experienced may have caused you to do or say something that could damage your relationship with them.

Youth Definitely with Bill, I owe him an apology. I also need to talk with my father, but I don't know how.

Rabbi It will come. Once you have truly accepted why you reacted as you did, you should take steps to remedy the relationships. This may involve an apology, or more specific response. If you feel resistance or embarrassment in admitting why you responded the way you did, it's a signal that the process of acceptance is not yet complete.

Youth This is truly amazing. I had no idea that I could learn all this from one blow up at a co-worker. There is so much more I need to think about . . . being responsible, blaming others, not accepting others when they don't fulfill my expectations . . . it's hard to face.

Rabbi You are experiencing the opening of your mind that comes with resolution. You can use every experience of conflict in the same way. Each holds a key to how and why you function the way you do. Each will reveal areas of darkness and ignorance in you, each will teach you about your relationship to others and the world around you.

Youth It's a great learning tool.

Rabbi Yes, it is. The more truth you accept about who you are, the less preoccupied in defending "your way", the more freedom you will experience in responding to life. As you work with this process, it will eventually condense into three simple steps: First, *awareness* of the negative emotion experienced. Second, *what am I refusing to accept?* Third, *acceptance & remedy.* Whenever you feel resistance rising up within you, in whatever form, remember these three simple steps to acceptance and resolution. Practice them in the moment. Observe your reactions to life. They will teach you everything.

Youth   Thanks. It's a great gift.

Rabbi   As you master acceptance of reality and take responsibility for your own state of being by using this process, you will experience less tension, more energy, vitality, health, hope and a sense of well being in your life.   It's like a low-grade headache or toothache which has persisted for many days. You become conditioned so that you hardly know the pain is there. But when it is totally removed, there is an enormous sense of relief, new energy emerges and your entire state of being is transformed. This is exactly the same when you have totally resolved a conflict in your life.

Youth   Do you mean every conflict in my life? Even the small ones?

Rabbi   Yes. Your personal example appeared to be a minor incident in your life. But even the most seemingly trivial irritations in life can be a great source of self-knowledge. In fact, it is often these apparent minor life situations which we tend to gloss over and not deal with. Yet, if unresolved, they begin to gnaw at our perceptions. We unconsciously start a data-gathering effort, accumulating incidents which support and justify our negative feelings. Soon, a major rift in the relationship develops, anger erupts over some minor incident which is out of proportion. Then a shopping list of complaints and incidents is trotted out to justify our negative behavior and blame the other person. It is much more difficult at this point to make sense of the complexity. If this happens, focus on one incident only and follow it to resolution. This will give you the insight to separate and resolve the other issues or incidents.

Youth   I can see this will take time.

Rabbi   Yes, the resolution process takes time to learn. But you have a lifetime. At first it will be like learning to ski or golf or ride a bike. Persistence through trial and error will eventually yeald a level of mastery. Sometimes, an incident which enrages us will not abate even though we know the answers to the above process. It may take several days to finally come to the acceptance of the situation and resolution. You will always know, however, if the process is complete by whether or not you can discuss it openly with others without any embarrassment or negative emotion arising.

Youth   What if I still can't get to resolution?

Rabbi   There is a second process of resolution that you may want to explore. It involves writing. I have used this process myself several times when confronted by a difficult situation or when I cannot get to full acceptance and resolution.

First, write about the incident or person that is bothering you. Don't censure your writing, you're not going to send it to them. Picture the person or incident and write with all the emotions which you would aim at them in person, if you could. This works for living or deceased persons who are the focus of your attention. There is a catharsis which takes place in simply writing out your emotions. Read and re-read what you have put on paper. Make sure it expresses everything you want to say.

Second, take another piece of paper and place it next to your writing. Read each sentence again and, as you do, write the impressions and thoughts which come immediately to mind on the second paper, as though you were having a dialogue with a very wise person who knows you better than yourself. Ask yourself the questions you don't want to hear! Ask what you are refusing to accept! Don't censure the responses, just write them down.

Third, you may be supprised at the answers you just received. Now, write on a third piece of paper the responses and thoughts which come to you as you read the second paper. Answer the questions posed. Be honest, direct. Gradually, you will uncover the causes and sources of your initial conflict and resistance. Repeat step three if you need further insight. The *acceptance* and *remedy* steps described in the first process are exactly the same.

Youth   That's a useful alternative. I'll try it as well.

Rabbi   I'm reminded of a teaching of Lao Tzu, "If everyone treated his heart as Teacher, who would be the only one without a teacher?" Intention is everything. Uncovering areas of ignorance within ourselves requires a *decision* that you will act on the answers received. The intention and desire to gain self knowledge and the faith that you can and will deal with everything uncovered, is crucial. Strong intention is an act of the will. It serves to galvanize us into action. It calls into our service the full capacities of our soul, which is always in touch with reality and is always orientated to assisting us in attaining our highest possibility. Remember, each of us only understands in others that which he first understands in himself.

Youth   Again, I need to think about everything I've learned today. It's amazing how each week that we meet, I go away feeling filled by new thinking and new perspectives. Can we meet next week?

Rabbi   Of course. ❏

Chapter

IV.

IDENTITY

"When one has become fascinated with something -- a problem, a person, a book, a scene -- then the object of fascination fills a person's experience and nothing else exists for him. This is the case, for example, in "true dialogue" between persons. The participants in dialogue are "fully there" -- their thoughts are not preoccupied with unfinished business, or fantasy that is irrelevant to the ongoing conversation."

Sidney Jourard

Chapter IV.

IDENTITY

Rabbi It's nice to see you again. How have you been this past week?

Youth Well, up and down. After our discussion about my angry response to Bill, my co-worker, I went to see him. I apologized for my outburst and told him a little of what I learned about myself. He was grateful, I think, because he was feeling guilty for not remembering to cover me while I was gone. My response helped both of us, so the relationship is restored.

Rabbi Did you talk with your father?

Youth Yes. We had a really good talk about a wide range of subjects. I think it was the best and most difficult conversation I ever had with him. I thought a lot about our relationship and ended up doing some writing before we met. I used the method you suggested last week and it was very helpful in sorting out my feelings about him. I tried to share with him what my experience as a child was like, but without blaming him or telling him he was wrong. He got defensive a few times, and so did I . . . but what I realized is that he was *there* in relationship with me, in that moment. That he had tried his best in providing for our family and it took a lot of his time away from where he would rather have been; that the past was gone – like spilt milk. My objecting to that would not add to the present moment and I had an opportunity to re-establish a different relationship with him, as an adult. So we are going fishing in Canada next month.

Rabbi   That sounds wonderful.

Youth   Yeah, I'm really looking forward to it.

Rabbi   So, what shall we talk about today?

Youth   You know, I feel like a load has been removed from me as a result of what I learned about myself . . . and in talking with Bill and my Dad. It's amazing how one little incident can trigger such an impact. I'm not sure what's going on, but I feel a need to learn about all the subjects we talked about . . . like I'm thirsty. Why?

Rabbi   You're experiencing resolution. Whenever you resolve a conflict in your life it gives rise to new perceptions and understandings about your motivation, behavior and relationship with others. It's like cleaning out your garage after several years of accumulating the junk of life. New space opens up, a sense of order and possibility emerges. Now you have room for something new. Each successive experience of resolution clears more inner space, enlarges your capacities of perception and response.

Youth Yeah . . . that's what it feels like.

Rabbi And just like a new, clean garage gives rise to longings to fill it with something you always wanted, like a new car or mountain bike, so too the new *inner space* created by clearing away the impasses in your life will give rise to new interests. Those interests are often the expression of an inner need that requires your attention . . . like nutrients needed by the acorn. The need for a new framework, a new way of thinking, within which to process the experiences of resolution, is common.

Youth What do you mean a new framework? A new way of thinking?

Rabbi I'm talking about a completely different orientation in one's life, a fundamentally *different* way of thinking and functioning. It involves the movement from an "I-centered" paradigm to a "reality-centered" paradigm. It involves the process of *disillusionment* that we talked about last week.

Youth I guess that's some of what I went through this past week.

Rabbi Exactly . . . you became disillusioned about how you functioned and avoided responsibility. It's very common. As children and adolescents the *world* is centered around ourselves. This is a natural process that enables us to establish our identity and *survive* in the physical, emotional and cultural environment we grew up in. Its like the chick that needs the shell of the egg to protect it during critical development stages. Eventually, the shell will suffocate the chick if it doesn't break through into a new world. We are the same. The *shell* of egocentricity that we built as a result of our journey to adulthood, is now what gets in the way of becoming our highest. *Negative emotions are the signal that we are bumping up against our shell of self-centeredness.*

Youth   So, when I'm in conflict or angry, its a signal that my ego is involved? That I'm self-involved?

Rabbi   Yes. Remember what conflict is? The refusal to accept reality. Your expectations about the *way it ought to be*, or the *way you think it is*, is a part of your self-orientation. *Yourself* is getting in the way of seeing clearly. The problem is that this frame of reference is based on the *illusion* that the world revolves around *you*, that *you* are the center. The movement from adolescence to maturity is the process of breaking down this *illusion*. It's learning how to accept the reality that *you*, the part that says "I am", is simply a small part of a much bigger whole, and that this whole does not depend on you for its existence.

Youth   Yes, I can see how that might work. I definitely had an idea of how things should have been with Bill and with my father, which was . . . my illusion I guess. You certainly helped me get disassociated from it!

Rabbi   Moving from illusion to reality may sound simple and obvious, but its not. As adults most of us never totally accept this. Oh sure, on an intellectual level we understand that we are totally dependent on our environment. Yet we continue to plunder that environment as though we aren't dependent. That's illusion. On a psychological level many of us are still arrested in the adolescent stage where we want, or refuse to give up, the being right about *our way* or *our ideas* when confronted with change and diversity. It's called egocentricity.

Youth   I have a boss at work who doesn't listen very well, who thinks he always knows best, who wants to flaunt his authority all the time. It's very hard to work with him. He wants the credit when things work, and blames others when they don't.

Rabbi   His self-involvement, which you experience as arrogance, is the mask he wears to hide a great insecurity. He doesn't know who he is, where he is, or where he is going.

Youth   What do you mean? I don't understand.

Rabbi   Every human has a center, a soul, an essence which is always in touch with reality. Its language is intuition and impressions which inform our mind and heart when we are open and receptive. It helps guide us along a path toward fulfillment of our highest, just as the acorn is guided in becoming the oak tree. Our self-orientation, our shell of who we think we are, is what gets in our way. To the extent we are preoccupied with ourselves, our possessions, our ideas, our opinions, our image . . . to that extent we lose connection with our center and the guidance it provides. We become lost.

Youth   But what did you mean when you said he didn't know who he is or where he is?

Rabbi   Aristotle once said, "The true nature of anything is the highest it can become". The oak tree is the true and highest nature of the acorn. What is the true nature of the human? What is *your* true nature? What is *your* highest? The great men and women throughout history give us a glimpse of the innate capacities of *all humans*, including you and me. Fulfillment of our highest potential is the built-in capacity, the birthright, of every human. It's part of the *structure* and *process* built into humans, just as the oak is in the acorn. So long as our needs are met, physical, mental, emotional and spiritual, we will *automatically* move toward our highest, pulled by what interests and delights each of us, and shaped by the experiences that our particular journey brings. That is . . . unless we get in the way of that process through our self-involvement, our egocentricity.

Youth   So are you saying that my boss is so wrapped up in himself that he has become lost to his higher potential?

Rabbi   Yes, in a way. I don't know your boss and therefore don't know the particular journey he has taken to his present state of being. But all of his behaviors you described are designed to keep the world out, to protect him. They are what worked for him, they are the shell that protects him from his fears, his insecurities. So long as he remains stuck in those negative behaviors, he is lost to a higher possibility.

Youth   I see. So what I am seeing in his behavior is not his true self, it's a mask he hides behind. Right?

Rabbi   It's the personality he has adopted to cope with his world. Of course, he is not aware of anything beyond himself because that is what fills his consciousness. Himself. There's no room for a higher expression, there's no room for love.

Youth   It's sad in a way. I never thought I'd feel sorry for him. He's so difficult to work with.

Rabbi   Your empathy is a result of your growing knowledge. Its good . . . it allows *understanding* to replace judgement or criticism. When you see in others that which you know in yourself, compassion and empathy are a result. You don't feel so separate from them, even if they are a pain in the ass at times.

Youth   I guess I can see him in some of my own behaviors as well. Its not pretty, but true. What did you mean when you said there's no room for love?

Rabbi   Love is a term that is almost meaningless in today's world. Love is an outcome of taking responsibility in one's life, of maturity, of functioning from your center.

Youth   You mean like empowerment?

Rabbi   That too is an overused term, but close to what I
mean. Empowerment is the capacity to align ourselves with a
purpose, goal or direction which transcends our private,
restricted, egocentric life. It is the quality of *responsiveness* to
change and the ability to maintain the initiative in those
situations. People who feel *empowered*, whether at work, or at
home, or in their community, have the sense that they matter,
that they make a difference and that they are able to respond to
whatever circumstance might unfold. George Bernard Shaw
observed that the true joy in life is, "The being used for a
purpose recognized by yourself as a mighty one. The being a
force in nature, instead of a feverish, selfish little clod of
ailments and grievances complaining that the world will not
devote itself to making you happy." He was of the opinion
that his life belonged to the *whole community*, that as long as
he lived, it was his privilege to do for it whatever he could.
That is a statement of identity, empowerment and love.

Youth   Yes . . . its very powerful. How can I empower my
friends or fellow workers to be more responsible? More
productive at work?

Rabbi   You can't. You cannot empower another person, just
as you cannot empower an acorn to become an oak tree. If
you think you can, you're in illusion. You can influence, but
not empower. You cannot empower a child to become a great
athlete, a college professor, scientist, artist or Rabbi. For the
more you try to manipulate the outcome of a child's life, the

more resistance, overt or suppressed, they will choose. Ultimately, you can only provide an *environment* that meets the child's needs and provide options, choices and standards of conduct; *they choose* the responses to the experiences life brings to them. With adults it's the same . . . you can be an *example* of the kind of behaviors you wish to encourage. By your actions, you enable and give power to an environment of openness, inclusiveness, respect, cooperation, honesty, integrity and responsibility. A single person can be a powerful agent for change . . . indeed, it's the only thing that can.

Youth So it starts with me, again? I'm beginning to hear a familiar refrain. How do I achieve a sense of empowerment in my own life?

Rabbi Empowerment, maturity, responsiveness, self-actualizing . . . all are terms to describe a *state of being.* You can't go after a state of being as a goal, because that goal is itself, self-oriented and egocentric . . . you can't get there from here. The process we are describing is a movement from being unconscious of who we are, as infants, to being terribly conscious of ourselves, as children, adolescents and young adults, to *forgetting* ourselves as we interact and respond to life, which is maturity. The later state is one in which we have become so preoccupied with *the other* that we forget ourselves and simply function.

Everyone has experienced this state of being, when you have become so intensely interested in your child, or work or planting a tree or talking with your father, that *you* become *lost in the experience.* The only thing that exists, in that moment, is responding and interacting with whatever or whoever is the focus of your attention. It is the becoming *unselfconscious* by being totally absorbed in the act of responding to life. You become one with the object of your attention.

Youth   My conversation with my father was like that. I didn't realize until later that we had talked for over two hours. It seemed like minutes, like nothing else existed.

Rabbi   Exactly. This is also an aspect of *love*, which is the highest function of the human. As you resolve your inner state of being and gain self-knowledge, you will become less defense, more settled in who you are. You are able *to forget yourself* and focus on what interests and delights you. You become preoccupied with the *other*, that which is outside yourself and has meaning to you.

Youth   Do you mean following my dreams? Things which I'd like to do with my life? Accomplish in my life?

Rabbi   Exactly. In establishing a purpose, goal or direction which transcends your personal life, in becoming totally preoccupied with it, you become *transformed* by the process of responding. The focus, however, must be on something beyond yourself; something which interests and delights you, something which *captures* your attention and fills you with satisfaction. The sense of *falling* in love is the experience of *losing* oneself into something of great value . . . the *other* without which you cannot live. So choose wisely. All of these experiences move us in the direction of responding to life, of moving beyond ourselves. Eventually, you will come to an awareness that you are simply a *capacity to respond* to what life is asking of you in any moment. Or, more deeply, you become the instrument through which life expresses its capacity to *love*. That's what it means to be truly human.

Youth   Wow, that's a *very* different definition of love than I've heard before. What keeps us from realizing this, from functioning this way?

Rabbi   We each choose the outcomes in our life.

Youth   What do you mean?

Rabbi   Each person inherits both positive and negative tendencies, strengths and weaknesses. They are like two sides of a coin that you can't separate, they are part of the same piece. Motivation is that which rouses the mind or spirit to activity. When we are motivated by self-interest and egocentricity, the illusion that "I" am the center, our actions are based on *power* and *control*. Outcomes of these actions lead to conflict, violence and alienation in relationships, because their nature is based on getting *my way*. When we are motivated by something of great value which transcends ourselves, our actions are focused on the attainment of that *value*, on bringing *it* to fruition. We become preoccupied with the *other*. Outcomes of these actions deepen and reinforce a sense of meaning in our lives because we are participating in something of value beyond ourselves.

Youth   So you are saying that we have only two choices again?

Rabbi   Yes. We choose which side of that coin motivates and interests us. One choice is reality-centered, one is illusion-centered; one is based on love and one is based on greed and power; one leads to empowerment, one leads to alienation; one leads to good and one leads to evil in the world. The choice is ours. On our journey from childhood to adulthood, we experience and experiment with both motivations. We learn about their outcomes in the world and upon ourselves; what works and doesn't work. As we move through the stages of adulthood, we tend to center our actions around one or the other behaviors, which becomes our predominant *set toward action*, our dominant motivation and identity. It doesn't mean we don't go back and forth, depending on the specific situation. But, ultimately we choose one or the other orientations to life.

Youth   Does this explain why its harder to change the older we get? Is this what it means to become set in our ways?

Rabbi   Yes. We choose behaviors that work for us in our environment. The longer we persist in those behaviors, the more a part of our identity they become, the more we resist something new, resist change. Have you ever tried to change a habit?

Youth   Yes, its hard. It's almost like my old behavior has a life of its own, like when I changed my diet last year.

Rabbi Persistence and faith are required to make changes in our life. Moving to a reality-centered orientation in one's life, to the *committed* life, is not easy, especially at first. But the rewards are great. The sense of responding to the life processes emerging in and around us; of participation in a much larger drama, a story we share with the entire life community of earth, the sense of centeredness and fulfillment . . . is an enchantment beyond words.

Youth That's very moving. . . . What did you mean by the *committed life*?

Rabbi Everything worthwhile requires commitment. If you want to become a great athlete, musician, teacher, entertainer, carpenter, librarian . . . all require commitment, effort and sacrifice. Commitment and action are what turn a positive thought into a permanent reality in one's life. If you want to attain your highest, it requires everything of you . . . nothing less will do.

Youth That sounds beyond my capabilities. What do I commit to? How do I do that?

Rabbi Life never asks more than you can handle, no matter how it seems in the moment. Becoming *disillusioned* is the first step . . . learning that you are not the center, the realization that there must be *more* to life than you see or know. You have already begun that process. Recall the way to resolve conflict in one's life? It is the *means* by which we remove the restrictions and impediments of egocentricity by *committing*, in advance, to resolve them. Conflicts and upsets *resolved* provide a window through which we gain self-knowledge and empower our full capacities as humans. As you do these things, new horizons, new ideas, new interests will emerge in you. Follow them, pursue them, love them. And as you do, life will bring to you more challenges, more conflicts, more opportunities . . . these are your teachers, your guides toward fulfillment.

Youth   You mean it's that simple? That's all?

Rabbi   Simple, but not easy. Consciousness is irreversible. Once you know something, you can't not know it. You may suppress it, forget it or ignore it, but it's there. Once the way toward fulfillment is known, tension is created between new possibilities glimpsed and the existing reality that you are living with. This dynamic tension is a consequence of knowledge. It's called *cognitive dissonance*. It can only be relieved by acting on what you already know, acting on the truth.

Youth   Do you have an example?

Rabbi   If I want to become a good golfer, I must learn the basic skills and then practice and practice. Practice is necessary to train mind and body in coordinated action so it becomes *automatic*. If I stop playing for a year or so, I have to re-train the muscles and mind to again permit the automatic functioning, but I never forget the basics. Gaining proficiency in golf is a part-time effort for most of us and therefore difficult to master. But *relationships* make up a constant fabric of your life, no matter where you are. If you begin to see that every relationship, with yourself, your family, community and workgroup, is an *opportunity* to learn and practice initiative, responsiveness, resolution, love . . . then it soon becomes automatic. Eventually this functioning will become part of your identity, a natural part of your existence, because *it works*. Committing to an empowered life, a religious life, is also like becoming a parent: a process is unleashed which you must facilitate, guide and honor, but which you cannot control or structure to your own desires.

Youth   What do you mean, a *religious* life? I'm not religious.

Rabbi   Everyone has a religion. It's what guides your actions in the world . . . your values, conduct, character and consciousness. You can always tell a person's religion by how they *function*. Their actions and attitude reveal the truth about who they are, no matter if they are Jew, Christian, Muslim, Hindu or any other sect. Our beliefs are largely irrelevant if they are not congruent with our functioning. One cannot speak of loving God, while exercising power and control over ones neighbor. The word *religion* comes from the Latin, *religio*, meaning "to bind back to the source". So religion is a way of life which calls us to our highest, to identify with the Source of all that is, to become part of the stream of existence which emerges in and around us moment by moment. We represent that presence on earth, we are part of that unbroken chain of existence stretching back to stardust. We must wake up to that reality.

Youth   So everything we have discussed over these past weeks is part of that picture? It's all part of a religious process? A value process? A life process?

Rabbi   Exactly. The names we use to describe that process are not important, but the realization of the *totality* of it all . . . that is what is important and meaningful. We must encourage others to follow that path, no matter how they identify themselves. We need to develop a new kind of human, one that identifies with the life process of this planet, with the community of beings that are its expression, with all humans, with our common journey and our common destiny. We must celebrate our diversity, our differences, our uniqueness as a source of strength and creativity to meet the challenges we will face together. That is the great work we are called to at this time.

Youth   I'm not sure I can do that. I don't have the experience or wisdom to know where to start or what to do. Your words speak to my heart, I know they are true . . . but what can I do?

Rabbi   If you hear the message, you have the capacity. Follow your heart, listen to what you have learned. That's all you need.

Youth   I'll think about that. See you next week. ❏

Chapter

V.

OTHERS

"There is nothing more difficult to take in hand, more perilous to conduct, or more uncertain in its success than to take the lead in the introduction of a new order of things."

Niccolo Machiavelli

Chapter V.

OTHERS

Rabbi   I'm sorry for being a bit late.

Youth   No problem. It gave me a chance to rethink our conversations. You have a way of framing things in a very big way; a way I find hard to relate to sometimes. When I think about my daily life, it's hard to see how it fits into a larger perspective. I mean, I live with people who have no idea of what we have discussed, who have never been exposed to these ideas. My neighbors, friends, co-workers . . . it doesn't impact their lives at all. It's hard to see how this new way of life can make a difference.

Rabbi   Everything takes time. The relationships you speak of, are all there is. That's where you are, that's where you start. Your life can't be separated from the lives of others or from the life process.

Youth   Yes, I know. I understand that. But how . . .

Rabbi   No, you don't see or understand, otherwise the question would not arise. You are always in relationship . . .

with your environment, with the life that surrounds you, with your friends and neighbors. We can never *not* be in relationship because that is how we define who we are. All knowledge, indeed everything in existence, depends on its relationship to everything else, including the capacity to understand our very existence. You cannot even *know* that *you* exist except in relationship to a greater existence in which you find yourself. Through our inquiries into the nature of matter, energy and consciousness we are learning that the only things which exist *are* relationships. Everything is defined and supported by everything else.

Youth So how does this relate to my question?

Rabbi It's a matter of appreciating all relationships, of seeing immense value in them. That's where conflict arises, where learning and possibility emerge. All conflict is a result of relationships, as we have learned. It arises in yourself as an objection or resistance to something which has already occurred. That objection is your internal response based on *meanings* you have constructed about the world outside yourself. We humans are utterly subjective in our experience of the world. Like the iceberg that is ten percent above water and ninety percent underwater, we attribute meaning and significance to our experiences and store them away underwater in our sub-conscious, so we are not even aware they exist. Then an incident happens which triggers an automatic response based on those meanings. The problem is the meaning and significance we have constructed about

objective incidents may, in fact, have no significance at all. . .
or a different significance than we imagined.

Youth   I don't understand how we create meaning from
incidents in our lives. How does it relate to conflict?

Rabbi   First, an incident happens, or does *not* happen as you
expect, which is an objective reality. It simply occurred. We
attach *meaning* to the incident based on what this kind of
event means or reminds us of. It triggers a response from our
past, which leads to unconscious data-gathering of other
incidents to justify our conclusion or positions. This leads to
alienation and conflict.

Youth   You mean like the incident with my father?

Rabbi   Yes. The meaning you attached about your father not
being at your ball games is a good example. He was simply
not there, that's all. You attached a meaning . . . that he must
not love you. The reality of his not being there is an objective
reality, it didn't mean *anything*. You gave it meaning, that is
the subjective process, the human process. You then found
other incidents that confirmed your conclusion, which built a
wall of alienation in the relationship. That wall was
constructed in your mind from the bricks and mortar of past
experiences and what they meant to you. By meeting with
your father, by sharing your separate experiences, you were
able to uncover some of the unconscious iceberg of your own
conditioning. In a way, it had nothing to do with him, but
without him you may never have learned that lesson.

Youth   So *I* was the one that created the rift in our relationship? None of it was his doing? Is that what you're saying?

Rabbi   Can you catch yourself in resistance right now? Not wanting to be totally responsible?

Youth   Yeah, I feel anger at the idea. I don't want to accept that thought.

Rabbi   Exactly. As you work through this resistance, you will see that you are responsible for all the meanings and conclusions you made as a child and youth. Some were accurate, some not. It's the way it is.

Youth   So how do I sort out the accurate from the illusion?

Rabbi   By the process we have been discussing for weeks. By what you did just now, in confronting your own resistance, and letting it go. The subjective nature of how we process and store information in the conscious and subconscious mind is important in understanding conflict and upsets with others. When you experience conflict and project it into a relationship by blaming another person, the result is a *dispute*. Blaming may also contribute to the other person defending themselves, which is an automatic survival response. Conversely, if someone directs their conflict, anger, sarcasm, hostility, at you, your survival response may lead to the same result. The issue in any upset with another is to first resolve your own state of being so that you see more clearly what is needed in the moment. This must be done unconditionally; it can never depend on the other person doing anything.

Youth   Why not?

Rabbi   Because your state of being is your responsibility, not theirs. Secondly, you now have the knowledge to resolve your inner condition. Responsibility is a consequence of knowledge.

Youth   I see. That's part of what I'm feeling, the not wanting to be responsible for what I now know. Maybe that is part of growing up, becoming an adult.

Rabbi   Yes it is. As your state of resistance, your conflict, is resolved the level of tension between you and the other person will diminish, because you are not feeding negative energy to it. You become free to exercise an appropriate response, which may involve an apology, or acknowledging the other person or simply listening. Be appropriate. This remedy is possible only because you have accepted your role in the dispute. It doesn't depend on the other person doing anything or resolving their emotions. However, by your actions, change of attitude and lack of hostility, the other person's natural defense mechanisms will diminish. They no longer feel threatened by you or the situation and become free to exercise their own initiative.

Youth   Yeah, I saw that happen in Bill when I began sharing some of what I learned about the incident.

Rabbi   When you act out of anger and frustration, your actions will almost always be inappropriate for the moment; they will expand incidents and encourage disputes. By taking responsibility for your own attitude, you are able to resolve disputes in which you are a participant quickly and effectively. It defuses the matter and gives permission to the other person to reduce their level of emotion. Things calm down. Alternatives can be explored and a settlement worked out rationally. Resolving your emotions, acknowledging your part in the incident and taking initiative toward resolving the dispute are powerful motivators for others to follow. When you capitulated the being right about Bill in your work situation, the emotional tension between you abated. You were able to restore a relationship. The *invisible field* of conflict and tension between you was gone. In its place was not only a sense of relief in both of you, but perhaps sense of closeness as though you had been through a mutual struggle, a shared experience, and come out whole. Is that right?

Youth   Yeah, now that I think about the incident, its effect on our relationship, the resolution, that's how I experienced it. You could actually see the tightness in his face go away, he relaxed. I guess he thought I was going to attack him. It was like a wall came down, and something we both experienced could be resolved.

Rabbi   Our ability to relate and work with others toward common interests and goals determines our effectiveness in the world. So it makes sense to develop skills in resolving the upsets and disputes in those relationships, which inevitably occur. Of course, to be most effective in this practice requires the insight and self-knowledge gained through direct experience in resolving ones own state of being. The ancient admonition, "Physician, heal thyself" is most appropriate.

Youth   But all relationships aren't the same. I don't know my neighbor well enough to share the insights I did with Bill or my father.

Rabbi   Yes, you're right. Resolution with others depends on the nature of the relationship. In a committed relationship such as a marriage, total honesty and integrity is appropriate because we have given each other *permission* for this level of dialogue. That's what a marriage commitment is all about. That same level of honesty may not be appropriate with your neighbor, however, because there is no permission between you. Your neighbor might be offended if you told her you didn't like the style or color of her hair. Your spouse may not like it either, but your feedback is accepted because of the relationship.

Youth   Yes, I can see that's true.

Rabbi   Relationships vary in kind, like concentric rings spreading outward in a pond. At the center is *family*. By this term I don't mean our genetic family. I am referring to those relationships in which a *commitment* exists. Marriage is a primary arena in which we learn about the implications of commitment. By this I mean coming to a place in a marriage where one can say to the other "there is nothing you could do or say that will cause me to leave the relationship". This is a very different level of commitment than we see in the world. It is an expression of unconditional love. It gives permission for complete honesty and integrity; it bestows freedom on the other to *be* themselves completely; it liberates the spirit. It doesn't mean there aren't conflicts and upsets. If fact, that's a natural consequence of such commitment. Marriage has been called the gymnasium of the soul because that's where the true workout of the soul is. It's where we learn what a commitment to *one* means.

Youth What do you mean, a commitment to one?

Rabbi Changing instruments does not relieve one from the necessity of learning the musical scale. The underlying lesson is the same. Changing partners in a relationship does not relieve one from learning the laws of relationship and the meaning of commitment to one person.

Youth I see . . . that's a very different concept than I've heard before.

Rabbi Yes, it's a very ancient concept. If I desire a relationship with the highest, with truth, with God, I discover the nitty-gritty details of what that means in my day-to-day relationships. To the extent I continue to hold on to *my way*, I become alienated from those relationships; to the extent I *lose myself* into the other . . . I become the instrument through which that higher value can emerge. This is the meaning of the Great Paradox of Jesus, "Whoever shall save his life will lose it, but whoever shall lose his life, will find it". If your identity is organized around yourself, your image, your possessions, your ideas . . . it is self-referential, narrow, restricted and identified with what is transient in nature. On the other hand, by losing yourself into something of great value, in identifying with the larger life process of the earth, in becoming an instrument of something higher, you become identified with what is eternal in its nature. You discover who you really are.

Youth   This is a new concept, at least by today's standards, of both commitment and marriage. I'm engaged to be married in a few months and I don't know if I can make that kind of commitment. Half of all marriages end in divorce. It worries me.

Rabbi   I understand. The failure of so many marriages, the breaking up of families, the lack of commitment, values and morals is testament to a profound ignorance, an alienation from who we are and what we are called to do. Be not afraid of marriage or the kind of commitment I described. It will come. Use the tools you have been given to resolve every impasse in that relationship. Do that, the rest will follow.

Youth   I guess you're right. That's all I can do anyway.

Rabbi   *Family* also includes others who share a similar commitment. There is a Chinese proverb that says, "Things equal to the same thing are equal to each other". If I commit to a goal, say to establish a community arts council, and you also commit to the same goal, then we have established a commitment to each other through our relationship to the common goal; we have a *relationship commitment*. You can count on me to work for that goal and I can count on you. Through the experience of working together toward the goal, we deepen our knowledge, experience and relationship with each other. So to paraphrase the proverb, "People committed to the same goals are committed to each other". A *team* is comprised of people *committed* to the same goals and to working with each other to attain them, like a football team, a workgroup, or an educational foundation. The goal or vision is the organizing principle which helps order the specific responses and organization required to attain it.

Youth I wish we had that sense of a common goal at my work. It seems like the opposite at times. My boss has his own agenda, his department head has hers, and I don't know what the owners want, except to make money. It's hard to feel aligned in that environment, like a team.

Rabbi Yes it is. Yet many businesses are learning these lessons. The insights of science, that we talked of a few weeks ago, into the nature of our universe are changing how we understand, design, lead and manage organizations. The glue that will hold such organizations together and ensure flexibility in adapting to a changing environment, has to do with agreements. Agreements are the ground rules by which each member of an organization or team works with each other. They are a powerful means that maintain the relationship commitment.

Youth What kind of agreements are you talking about?

Rabbi There are four. The first one is, I will resolve all conflict in which I find myself; second, I will not blame others; third, I will maintain an attitude of goodwill; and fourth, I will work cooperatively with others toward our common goals.

Youth Perhaps you could explain why they are so powerful? Why do they work? I don't see how agreements I make can have an effect on others.

Rabbi These agreements are framed as a set of personal commitments of the individual. They are statements of *personal responsibility* that do not depend on others for their implementation. They are, therefore, very powerful in creating an atmosphere of trust, mutual respect, unity of purpose and empowerment. By committing to these agreements, people gradually learn their implications through the experience of working together, even if they had no exposure to the concepts before. Individuals can adopt these standards of conduct by themselves and still have a tremendous influence on others.

Youth Yeah, but can these really be used in a business?

Rabbi Yes. This set of agreements can be used in any relationship or group, such as a marriage, an educational or religious foundation, a community group . . . or a business enterprise. The only difference is the fourth agreement that is specific to the goals. Our common goals determine the depth to which our relationship extends. If you and I are committed to teaching conflict resolution, then we must demonstrate that capacity in ourselves. This goal requires a high degree of integrity and honesty between us, much like a marriage, so that every upset and every conflict is resolved. Otherwise, we have nothing to say about what we are teaching. In fact, it *is* a marriage in the sense we are committed to a common goal that has meaning and value to us. The higher the value of the goal, the deeper the relationship can extend. A *brother* or *sister* is one who is committed to the same values and goals in life and with whom we can share anything. It is a relationship of integrity.

Youth   I don't know of any group or organization that works that way. I can see that my workplace would be an entirely different, a better place, to work if we adopted those agreements. But what about my friends? I don't see them adopting these agreements.

Rabbi   They don't have to. *Friends* are persons with whom you share interests or experiences but which may not have the same values or goals. You may have many friends with whom you enjoy golfing, skiing, or mountain biking; but you wouldn't consider them a *brother or sister* because the relationship is based on mutual activities, not mutual values and goals. This in no way diminishes the meaning of the relationship. Friendship is also defined by the level of *consent* we give each other for honest dialogue. You may have a very close relationship with your real brother, sister, aunt, uncle, but if there is no *consent* for mutual integrity in the relationship, then this defines a different kind of relationship. I may give you consent for complete honesty and feedback in our relationship, but if you don't act on this commitment or do not welcome the same level of honesty in return, then the sense of integrity, of unimpaired wholeness in the relationship, cannot be established. We are friends, but not family.

Youth   I never thought about different kinds of friendships, but I guess you're right. I can be totally honest with my fiancée and, maybe one other friend, but that's it. My other friends are simply not interested in that much honesty. We like common activities, but not much more.

Rabbi   The last category of relationship is *neighbor*. Neighbors include all those not in the first two categories. They include acquaintances, business associates, people we meet in our journey through life. They also include those we have never met, because we share the common neighborhood of life. To the extent you can transcend your self-orientation and gain self-knowledge, you come to realize that we all share the same journey, that we have much more in common than our differences. There are no strangers, there are no enemies. Conversely, if you remain stuck in your self-centeredness, demanding your way, alienated from others, then you will experience others as strangers, competitors and enemies . . . you descend into the world of opposites.

   Family, friend and *neighbor* are terms used to describe dimensions of commitment, consent, and integrity in our relationships. There are, in fact, no distinct lines between these categories. The quality and character of these relationships move back and forth depending on our journey and the experiences which that journey brings to us. It has been my experience that most of the people I would call *family*, though separated by distance and years, remain for a lifetime. When we get together with such people after years of separation the relationship is re-established instantly, as though it was only yesterday we shared our lives and goals together.

Youth   What did you mean by *the world of opposites*?

Rabbi   It is the world of binary thinking. This mode of thinking sees the world in terms of opposites: good vs. evil; right vs. wrong; light vs. dark; socialism vs. capitalism; conservative vs. liberal; my way vs. your way. It is rooted in our ancient animal instincts of survival . . . fight or flight, life or death. This way of thinking is automatic in childhood and adolescence because it helps us learn about the world by seeing differences and in defining ourselves. As we gain experience, we learn that reality is much more complex and that a new way of thinking is necessary to resolve the contradictions we observe. Our automatic response, based on *binary thinking*, is adversarial in nature; it's a limited view of reality.

Youth   So is there another mode of thinking?

Rabbi   Yes, we could call it integrative, systemic or holistic thinking. It is a way of focusing on what is both universal and unique simultaneously. It is seeing diversity as a collective strength not a problem, and everything as interconnected and interdependent. It is seeing that what affects one part, affects the whole. The difference between these two ways of thinking is like moving from a two-dimensional world on a flat surface, to a three-dimensional world where you gain perspective and can *see* more. The two-dimensional world is still there, but is enriched by another dimension of perception and understanding. It could also be likened to a change from black and white vision to color vision. There is a greater sense of *wholeness* and *clarity* to what we observe in the world, which brings new perceptions, deeper understanding, more choices, greater freedom.

Youth   I have often wondered about the significance of the person who risks his or her life to save that of a stranger. Where does that fit in the categories of relationships you outlined? Whether rescuing someone from a burning building, jumping into icy waters to save a person from drowning in swift currents, or the many other heroic acts of self-sacrifice; I ask myself why? How?

Rabbi   What do you think?

Youth   I don't have an answer. How could a person, in an instant of time, forget themselves completely to rescue another? Not only forgetting themselves, but also family, friends, all relationships and their entire future existence? When these people are interviewed later, their response is usually, "I didn't think of myself at all, only the person in trouble. I just reacted, as *anyone* would do"

Rabbi Well, not everyone. But this is a common enough occurrence that it is not unique in human experience; in fact it's quite common. Where do you think this capacity to surrender one's own life to rescue the other comes from?

Youth That's a great question. Perhaps it speaks of a much deeper connection than we suspect?

Rabbi Could it be that our soul recognizes no separation between ourself and the other? Are we each an integral part of a greater *sea of being* which organizes itself into the material reality we experience? Are we are truly *one,* but don't recognize it? Is our experience of space, time and life in part an illusion of our senses? I think so. Our understanding of matter, energy and consciousness point in this same direction. I am reminded of Alan Watts description of reality, "We are beginning to see matter not as energy or as a *stuff,* but rather as energetic pattern, moving order, active intelligence."

Youth That's amazing. It's almost like coming back to our first discussion. Realizing that all our new knowledge of how the universe works, is interconnected, is expressed in this one simple act of rescuing another.

Rabbi That's a good insight, a good way to put it.

Youth Its hard to think about such big ideas. I often wonder how the ideas of various religions can be resolved? Each has a

God concept, a Savior concept, a Teacher concept. Each follows different beliefs and practices. How can they all be true? Be resolved? Science is dethroning many of our cherished beliefs from the past. Will religions be next?

Rabbi You're asking a very big question. When thinking about these ideas myself, I recall a down-to-earth example I once heard which has been useful to my understanding. Have you ever encountered a snail in your garden? After picking the snail up and depositing it somewhere else, have you ever asked yourself what the snail knows of you? Or how it suddenly found itself in a new environment? In fact, you do not exist to the snail. It doesn't have the capacity to perceive much beyond heat, cold, light, dark, touch and maybe taste. . . but of human life or existence it knows nothing. The snail will never *know* anything of the human dimension; of art, science, literature, music, civilization or any other human activity. It simply does not possess the neural capacity or type of consciousness to even sense any of that exists. In fact, it does *not exist* to the snail. In that same sense, how do we humans know that dimensions of existence are not present within the universe which are as far beyond our human existence as we are beyond the snail?

Youth That's an interesting way to conceptualize our place in the universe.

Rabbi The fact that we cannot see, hear, taste, smell or sense those other dimensions of life directly, or indirectly does not mean they don't exist. Intuitively, we may even sense a dimension of life beyond our own, an intimation briefly glimpsed, but it's not yet in the realm of human knowledge. It also does not mean those dimensions don't exert a significant influence over our human dimension, just as you chose to make an abrupt change to the snail's life by moving it outside your garden. In fact, there is evidence to suggest this is closer to the truth.

Youth   I guess it really doesn't make any difference which religious tradition we follow. The cosmos is the way it is, regardless of how humans believe it to be.

Rabbi   In a way, that's right. Religions have been the repositories of values, traditions, knowledge and collective wisdom that has been invaluable to our species. They call us to a higher order, a higher level of functioning and to a relationship with the Highest. They provide a framework for our inner, spiritual development. Their understandings are intuitive in nature, yet their cosmologies are, in many ways, more in line with our new understanding of the universe.

Youth   I asked my aunt one day why she continued to be a practicing Catholic. She is a very bright, articulate and educated person, so I often wondered. She said, "Because it comforts me." As good an answer as I've heard.

Rabbi   Yes. We cannot underestimate the value of rituals and traditions in the life of our species. Instead of viewing them as something separate from science, we should regard their traditions and wisdom as insights into the nature of a reality science may not have access to.

The significance of our new knowledge and insight is only beginning to dawn upon us. At the center of it all is the idea that *relationships* constitute the basis of reality. We cannot separate ourselves from each other, no matter how hard we try. We're stuck. So why not make the best of it and discover how to improve the quality of *every* relationship we have . . . from the environment of life to the obnoxious neighbor next door. Resolving our state of being and the restrictions of our mind and heart opens a new world of possibilities never before glimpsed. We have within our grasp the capacity to resolve every relationship. It doesn't depend on the other person responding the way you want or expect; but it does mean you carry no ill will or regrets about the relationship. You are resolved about the relationship, that's what *resolution with others* truly means. Doing this religiously will bring a sense of meaning to one's life.

Youth   Thanks. See you next week? ❏

Chapter

VI.

JOURNEY

"The most beautiful emotion we can experience is the mystical. It is the power of all true art and science. He to whom this emotion is a stranger, who can no longer wonder and stand rapt in awe, is as good as dead. To know that what is impenetrable to us really exists, manifesting itself as the highest wisdom and the most radiant beauty, which our dull faculties can comprehend only in their most primitive forms—this knowledge, this feeling, is at the center of true religiousness. In this sense, and in this sense only, I belong to the rank of devoutly religious men."

Albert Einstein (1879–1955)

Chapter VI.

JOURNEY

Youth   Hi, Rabbi. How are you today?

Rabbi   Excellent, couldn't be better . . . it's a beautiful day.

Youth   I've been thinking about our last conversation, about relationships . . . my relationships. I realized that I avoid certain people because they have attributes I don't like . . . ones I avoid in myself. I also learned where it comes from.

Rabbi   Good. Do you have an example?

Youth   Yes, a woman at my work. I avoided her and didn't like being around her. It finally dawned on me that she reminded me of someone with similar traits: my mother. My mother was a very angry and bitter woman, who had been divorced since I was very young. She raised my brother and myself while working to support us. Life was hard and a burden to her, which she let us know often. She was also alcoholic. I adopted behaviors of avoidance and independence to cope with the emotional environment at home. Ah ha! I finally understood *why* I was avoiding the woman at my office. Her behavior reminded me of negative traits in my mother. I was unconsciously adopting the survival behavior of *avoidance* to cope with my own projections on her. I feared being *hurt* by her, which was my childhood fear of my mother. After realizing and accepting all this, I was able to establish a different relationship with my co-worker. I could finally *see* her differently.

Rabbi That's a good example. It reveals the importance of every relationship, why we like certain people and dislike others. When we replace judgement with understanding, it frees us up to relate in a different way.

Youth Yes, it was a real learning experience for me. I didn't realize how my past survival responses, as you put it, continue to operate in me today. It explains my reactions to other people in my life, why I like some and avoid others. I'll have to think about them . . . see what I can learn.

Rabbi Good. You're on your way. You have the tools for learning everything you need on your life's journey.

Youth That's comforting, but it feels like I'm setting sail into an unknown sea.

Rabbi In a way, that's right. But the journey is known, the way has been charted by others. The specific details of your journey, however, remain in your hands.

Youth What do you mean, the way has been charted by

others? How is the journey known?

Rabbi   Every human being, no matter their religion, culture or ethnic origin, is on a common journey. Everyone goes through the experiences of birth, childhood, adolescence, adulthood, maturity and eventually death. We could call this "every persons journey". You can think of it as a circle, representing wholeness, completeness. At the top of the circle is a point that represents our birth. The first quadrant of the circle is our journey from birth through childhood to adolescence to the point where we "leave home". During this period we are totally *dependent* on others including parents, family and teachers. We learn basic skills, explore interests and develop values and attitudes that guide our actions in surviving this period of life. Leaving home is often a two-stage affair, we leave home physically long before we leave emotionally. Many cultures mark this experience with ceremonial rights of passage, to mark the ending of one stage of life and the beginning of another.

Youth   I remember that part of my life well. I'm learning only now how much I am a product of those experiences.

Rabbi   It's an important part of everyone's life. It determines much of how we approach our journey. In the next quadrant, we venture into the world to establish ourselves *independent* from parents and family. We experience trials and ordeals which test our ideas of who we are. Often, we are in a state of rebellion against authority, to help establish our independence. We encounter mentors and helpers, which are somehow there when we need them. Eventually, we establish ourselves in the world, no longer dependent on family for our survival or the sense of who we are. We reach a point of *identity* where we can say, "I am a . . . teacher, architect, lawyer, carpenter, etc". We gain a sense of who we are by what we *do* in the world to sustain ourselves.

Youth   That's the portion I'm in now.

Rabbi   Right. Somewhere along this path of independence, as we experiment with various relationships, we find the *other* for whom we have been, unconsciously, searching. We establish a permanent relationship. We settle into a lifestyle that reflects our identity, values and economic means. We have children, establish a home, start accumulating the *stuff* that we need and want. This is a period of *interdependence*, where we have of our own choice, established dependency relationships with spouse, children and co-workers. Others now depend upon us . . . we are faced with issues of responsibility and commitment. Eventually, as we live the life we have chosen, there arise questions, "Is this all there is?"; "What must I do now?" We sense that *something* is missing, something unfulfilled . . . but what?

Youth   I recall a discussion with a very successful executive who described how he had gone after and achieved everything "they told me to do", as he put it, referring to parents, teachers, and mentors. He had attained everything in life he thought he wanted – success, money, family, material possessions, prestige, recognition . . . but he was not completely satisfied. He was questioning everything in his life.

Rabbi   It's a critical stage in a person's life, when we begin to question who we are, where we are going and what we must do. It usually occurs in the mid-thirties to mid-forties, but can be much earlier or later in one's life. Often we make radical changes to cope with the disillusionment, start a new career, get another degree, have another child, divorce, remarry, quit our job, etc..

Youth   Yes, I see that same pattern in many of my relatives and parents' friends.

Rabbi   When we have attained a level of comfort, when we have competency in the world, we often discover it's not enough. That sense of *something* being missing at this point in our journey comes from a lack of meaning and significance in ones life. We talked about this as our deepest need. This sense of malaise is actually good. It is an invitation to transform ourselves, it is the *call to adventure* encountered by hero's throughout time.

Youth   I read a book in college by Joseph Campbell that reminds me of this same journey. It sounds familiar.

Rabbi   Yes, his book, *The Hero of a Thousand Faces*, is similar to what we are talking about. Campbell described the universal journey of the hero, as depicted in the mythologies of civilizations throughout the world, which journey represents our innate capacities. The hero leaves home in response to the call to adventure. He encounters a shadow presence guarding a passage, beyond which he journeys through an unfamiliar world that threatens and tests him, some of which are helpers who give magical aid. The hero eventually undergoes a supreme ordeal and gains his reward or "boon", which is intrinsically an expansion of consciousness and being, illumination, transfiguration, freedom. The final work is the return home with the boon which restores his world.

Youth   So are we all heroes? Is that what every persons journey means?

Rabbi   In a way. The grand adventure described by Campbell is intimated by the journey of our lives. But we are responsible for choosing the outcomes, by the responses we make to what life brings us. We leave home, experience an unfamiliar world which threatens and tests us, we find teachers and helpers from whom we learn valuable lessons. Eventually we attain mastery and an identity in the world. Then we become disillusioned and embark on another phase of life to find what's missing and, if persistent and motivated, eventually receive the "boon", sense of purpose and fulfillment, which restores us. We then return "home" to assist others.

However, the fourth quadrant of this journey is an entirely new cycle of experience, like the hero's journey in itself. This part is accessible *only* by transcending ones self-orientation and committing to something beyond ourselves. It is a stage of *maturity*. Our human journey from birth to maturity is organized as if to guide us through predictable stages of *inner growth* so we eventually confront *who* we are and *what* we must do to claim our birthright.

Youth　What do you mean claim our birthright?

Rabbi　It involves claiming who we really are. Identifying with the highest we can become; becoming an instrument through which life expresses its capacity to respond and to love. That is who we are at our very center. That is the purpose of our journey through the stages of life.

Youth　Are these stages or cycles of human development universal? Do all people go through them?

Rabbi　Yes. The stages of dependence, independence, interdependence and maturity are universal. Not only do individuals move through these stages, but whole cultures and nations do as well. Generally, our species is still very young and in various stages of rebellion, of asserting our independence from the earth which nurtured our beginnings. That is part of our present crisis.

Youth　In a way though, this story comforts me. The fact that we are all on a similar journey together, that the way is known, like getting to the moon, removes a certain anxiety about the future. It helps me understand the issues I face at this stage of my life. But are you suggesting that this journey has an intention behind it?

Rabbi Of course. Intention is built into everything we observe in the universe. How else can you explain it? I choose to think of that intention as an attribute of God. But again, by whatever name you call it, however you approach it, there is no denying the underlying attributes of creation.

Youth What do you mean, underlying attributes?

Rabbi Everything in existence has a source, everything is connected. No matter what you observe, if you trace its origins, its connections back in time, you come to a mystery. Nothing sprang into existence by itself, but rather continuously emerges through the process of creation. That process has a direction, it moves from the simple to the complex, toward greater responsiveness, greater awareness, higher states of consciousness and complexity. At every level of observation, from the microscopic to the telescopic, there is displayed an incredible intelligence, an order and structure to existence of which we only glimpse the smallest fraction. Like the snail trying to understand how it was moved in the garden. It all expresses a will and intention that operates at every level and dimension of existence that we know.

Youth Is this what you are calling God?

Rabbi It's an expression of the same thing, no matter what we call it or how we relate to it. The problem with humans is that we have separated all this *totality* into separate pieces so we can study and understand it. In that process of separation we have lost sight of our connections and dependency . . . to

122

the universe, the earth, the life community . . . to each other. That separation is the source of our present ignorance.

Youth   Yes, I can see that we need a different orientation to everything. That's what we've been talking about for weeks, literally, a new way of life. Isn't it?

Rabbi   Precisely. Our thinking must change, our behaviors will follow. This is actually happening as new insights into the nature of the life system emerge. Experience gives rise to conflict and problems, from which we gain insight, which leads to knowledge, which leads to changes in our thinking and our cosmology. The difficult part is changing behavior. That's why we have spent so much time on the *inner journey* required to make those changes. That inner journey is what ultimately leads to a sense of meaning in one's life. It's our deepest need.

Youth   Meaning is a human need? Like food and water?

Rabbi   Yes. Abraham Maslow described his experiences in a Nazi concentration camp during World War II. in his book, *Man's Search for Meaning*. He depicted both the unbearable conditions endured by millions and the deep underlying, transcendent spirit of human beings which emerges when everything is literally stripped from one's life. What Maslow discovered, upon later reflection, is that the search for *meaning* and *fulfillment* is the deepest and most profound of human needs.

Youth   How would you describe fulfillment?

Rabbi   The term *fulfillment* suggests a task, purpose, duty or contract to be completed which, upon its completion, is satisfied. That sense of completed satisfaction of a task well done is what most people desire in life. Whether it be in relation to one's family, job, profession, community, synagogue or church, the experience of completion and closure which comes in attaining a goal or completing the task is very satisfying. Like a great thirst which is quenched. These experiences are also intimations that our life as a whole may have a purpose and intention which, if followed, brings a deeper sense of significance. It is, as Maslow discovered, one of the most profound needs of the human. To have the sense that one's life has had meaning. That somehow a great purpose has been working its way through the totality of our life experiences so that, in the end, we come to the quiet acceptance that there were no mistakes, that it all adds up, that there is a *meaning* and *significance* to it all.

Youth   That is a beautiful sentiment. I only hope I find that in my own life.

Rabbi   I hope so too. There is a quotation by John Elof Boodin that I brought with me today . . . you may find helpful. It speaks to what we have just discussed. "We do not understand, but somehow we are part of a creative destiny, reaching backward and forward to infinity . . . a destiny that reveals itself, though dimly, in our striving, in our love, our thought, our appreciation. We are the fruition of a process that stretches back to stardust. We are the material in the hands of the Genius of the universe for a still greater destiny that we cannot see. Nothing happens but what somehow counts in the creative architecture of things. The pangs of pain and failure are the birth-throes of a transition to better things. We are separated for a time by the indifference of space and by our blindness which isolates us. But in us is the longing for unity. We are impelled by a hidden instinct to reunion with the larger heart of the universe."

Youth   That captures what you have been teaching perfectly. Again, I have a lot to assimilate. See you next week?

Rabbi   Great. See you then. ❑

Chapter

VII.

LEADERSHIP

"Our deepest fear is not that we are inadequate. Our deepest fear is that we are powerful beyond measure. It is our light, not our darkness that most frightens us. We ask ourselves, who am I to be brilliant, gorgeous, talented and fabulous? Actually, who are you not to be? Your playing small doesn't serve the world. There's nothing enlightened about shrinking so that other people won't feel insecure around you. We were born to make manifest the glory that is within us. It's not just in some of us; it's in everyone. And as we let our own light shine, we unconsciously give other people permission to do the same. As we are liberated from our own fear, our presence automatically liberates others."

Nelson Mandella
1994 Inaugural Speech

Chapter VII.

LEADERSHIP

Youth   I have been thinking of our conversation last week and the stages of our journey you described. The four stages of dependency, independence, interdependence and maturity . . . do you recall?

Rabbi   Yes, indeed.

Youth   I am soon to be married. I have also been offered a supervisory position with my new company. I'm nervous about both. Does it mean I'm entering the third stage of the journey?

Rabbi   In terms of marriage, yes you are beginning a new phase of your journey. You are choosing a long-term relationship of interdependence. In terms of your job, that too involves interdependence. You must accomplish goals through the work of others, which depend on you for guidance, direction and leadership.

Youth   But why am I so nervous?

Rabbi   When you were young and first learned to ride a bike or climb a steep mountain face, were you nervous?

Youth   Yes . . . and excited at the same time.

Rabbi   Why?

Youth   It was new and unknown. I was afraid of failing, of being hurt, of looking foolish. But I knew that's what I wanted and plunged ahead until I learned. It was exhilarating.

Rabbi   Is your current nervousness similar?

Youth   Yeah, it is. I guess its fear of the unknown. I'm less nervous about my marriage, because I love her so much and want to be with her always. We enjoy each other's company and have similar interests and values. But taking on so much responsibility at work, that scares me more.

Rabbi   Why do you think so?

Youth   I don't know. I'm not sure I want the responsibility, I'm not sure I can supervise others to accomplish a common purpose. I like the added money and the perks that go with the position. But . . .

Rabbi   But what? You're in resistance, that's all. What are you refusing to accept?

Youth   That . . . I will be responsible for others, that I'm accountable. I can't hide. I don't know if I can be a leader.

Rabbi   It's a part of your journey, part of becoming who you really are. Leadership is an art to be learned over time. It involves the exercise of authority and responsibility.

Youth   What do you mean exercise authority?

Rabbi   Do you recall our discussion a few weeks ago about responsibility being a consequence of knowledge?

Youth   Yes, I do.

Rabbi   Knowledge comes from experience, raised to a level of understanding and meaning. Everything that lives has experience, even a tree. But only humans can think about their experiences, relate them to other memories, connect them to meanings we have constructed about the world and pass that knowledge to others through stories and words. When you really *know* something from your own experience, there is a sureness and sense of security that is its outcome. What are you really sure of?

Youth   Well, I know a lot about fly fishing because I've done so much of it. I'm sure about good equipment, reels, line, types of flies, how to tie them and which to use in different conditions and times of day. I guess that's an area I feel comfortable in.

Rabbi   Right. In relation to a novice at fly fishing, you have *authority* by virtue of your knowledge and experience. Its not your position, as a fishing guide, that gives you that authority. It's the level of knowledge and security you have about the sport, in guiding a novice along the learning curve of fly fishing. Do you agree?

Youth   Yes. I see that clearly when I take others along fishing. They soon ask me about everything I'm doing.

Rabbi   So the source of your authority has to do with knowledge, competency and your ability to produce outcomes in fishing. Your job is the same. You must have exhibited talent and initiative to be considered as a supervisor?

Youth   I guess so. I am always asking questions, trying to improve our workflow, checking out the competition, reading trade rags, trying new ways. I find it fun and challenging.

Rabbi   That's why they chose you. You exhibited initiative and leadership. You have already proven to others that you possess the potential to manage and work with others. Like the oak tree in the acorn, remember?

Youth   Yes, I guess you're right. Yet I'm uncomfortable being the boss over others I have worked with.

Rabbi   You're not *over* them. That's old thinking. If anything, you are *under* them. You are there to serve them as well as your company.

Youth   I don't understand. What do you mean, serve them?

Rabbi   A leader is one who serves others. A leader facilitates and coordinates the efforts of many into one. A leader recognizes and values diversity . . . of talents, skills and knowledge among people. He works to bring forth what is unique and valuable in each person. He facilitates cooperation, aids in resolving conflict and clarifies the vision and goals of the group or organization. That is part of what defines leadership.

Youth   That's a lot of responsibility. I don't know if I can do that, become that.

Rabbi   It's not a burden, it's a privilege. It is a profound blessing to be in a position to serve a greater whole, whether it be your family, community or company. The way we think about leadership determines what kind of leader we become.

Youth   That sounds familiar. Our thinking determines what we see and how we function, isn't that what we talked about before?

Rabbi   Yes it is. Leadership is a universal experience, we just don't recognize it for what it is. In our journey from childhood to maturity we experience many types of leaders. We learn about issues of authority, structure, control, responsibility, initiative from our parental environment. If that environment was dependable, if it was nurturing, was structured yet benevolent, we tend toward a positive relationship toward authority. We trust it. If our early environment was capricious, unstructured, hostile or threatening, we tend to develop a negative and rebellious relationship with authority.

Our relationship with authority is central to how we think about and exercise leadership. In our daily life we assume roles of husband, wife, father, mother, provider, nurturer, teacher and leader. They are all positions of authority; they are all *dependency* relationships that we have chosen . . . others now depend on us. And with dependency and authority comes *responsibility*. We are responsible for our actions, our attitudes, our responsiveness and ultimately, the outcomes of all relationships we are in.

Youth   So our environment helps determine our leadership style? The way we exercise authority?

Rabbi   Yes. The environment you choose as an adult also influences your thinking and behavior. The friends you associate with and the values they hold, influence you. The entertainment you choose, the books you read, the business environment you are exposed to . . . all have an impact on your consciousness. Everything is connected.

Youth   I guess I never thought about the effects of my relationships. Can you give me an example of how that works?

Rabbi   When you were a youth, what kind of friends did you choose?

Youth   It varied. One year I was part of the social group at school. We had a lot of fun, cut classes, went to parties, dances, things like that. It was fun to challenge authority, to see what would happen. Later, I found other friends who were more interested in school and learning. I felt challenged about grades and the fun of learning new things. I was also concerned about getting into college at that time and they helped me refocus my attention. I had one close friend throughout my teen years as well, we grew up near each other and liked the same things.

Rabbi   It sounds familiar. You were experimenting with various friends and social groups to learn about yourself. When you were in the social group, how did you behave?

Youth   Like the others. We enjoyed doing things together, I didn't really value school so much as I did later.

Rabbi   And did you engage in behaviors you wouldn't think of doing now?

Youth   Yes, many.

Rabbi   Why did you choose those behaviors at the time? Why did you not just say no? Why did you later choose a different group to be with? What kept you bonded with your long time friend?

Youth   I think I see where you're going. I was influenced by the group as a whole, I choose to conform with the values and energies of the group. Right?

Rabbi Exactly. Remember the story of the 100th monkey? When enough people focus on common things it creates a field of intention, a group consciousness, which helps bring others into alignment with that field. In physics its called *rhythm entrainment*. For example, you may have noticed on a balmy summer evening the fireflies settling in a bush, blinking on and off. At first this blinking is random, but fairly soon we notice that an order is developing. After a while the fireflies within the bush are blinking on and off in unison. It seems that nature finds it more economical in terms of energy, to have periodic events close in frequency occur in phase or in step with each other.

That's what cultures do, they inculturate individual members into alignment with the whole. In business, we talk about the culture of an organization. It's an important element in bringing alignment to a group. Leadership is involved in bringing alignment among people toward a common vision, around common values.

Youth I guess I wasn't much of a leader in my youth.

Rabbi In your youth, your behavior was aligned with the values and direction of each group of friends. You did not exhibit much individuality, you conformed. It's normal. Later in your life, you have more sense of yourself, are more secure in who you are and what you like, you are more freed up in exploring options. But there is still the pressure to conform with the culture of the organization, right?

Youth   Yes, I see that.

Rabbi   You were chosen for a leadership role within that organization because you exhibited initiative and responsibility. That comes from a level of self-knowledge.

Youth   How is initiative related to self-knowledge?

Rabbi   Initiative is the exercise of your will. Your will is what is necessary for action, in exploring your environment, in gaining experience and knowledge, it's a vital part in discovering who you are and what you can do. Whenever you find yourself in a place were you can't exercise initiative, you're in the wrong place.

Youth   What do you mean, wrong place?

Rabbi   When you are a student it is appropriate to be quiet and receptive in the presence of a teacher. You capitulate taking action or initiative in order to learn. Yet when a question arises and you don't understand something, initiative is required to ask the question. We move back and forth from initiative to rest, from action to quiet . . . its part of the rhythm of life. It is a movement and a rest, like your heart beating or a pendulum swinging. The key is in knowing when to exercise each capacity. Our birthright is to *see* and *respond* to our environment, to cooperate with the rhythms of life. Seeing requires rest, responding requires initiative. It's our built-in nature. So when you find yourself in a place where you cannot exercise your birthright, where you feel stifled and constrained, it is usually a signal that you are in resistance or in the wrong place. If in resistance, you know how to discover the cause and deal with it. If not resistance, but simply the structure or situation you are in, then your only choice is to accept that situation, surrender to it . . . then exercise initiative to move on.

Youth   That sounds like my last job. I was in a company that was very structured and my role highly defined. I saw many areas that could be improved, but my boss was not open. He felt safe the way things were and discouraged any initiatives I suggested. It made me feel not valued or appreciated. Others felt the same way, but accepted the situation. They were more interested in security than change. So, I eventually changed jobs.

Rabbi   It appears you made the right decision. Your co-workers had capitulated to the environment they were in. They choose a passive role because that is what the environment and culture demanded. There is nothing wrong with that choice . . . for them. But it was not the right environment for you. Your being chosen to assume a leadership role in your new company is evidence of that.

Youth   Yes, I can see that now. The management at my new company is much more open to change and possibility. They encourage change and innovation, both in our products, services and organization. I feel free, like I'm in the right place at the right time.

Rabbi   That's great. It sounds like an environment were you can experiment, make mistakes and learn from them. It's an environment were personal growth is encouraged and honored. You can see by your own example how crucial leadership is in shaping an environment which enhances performance of individuals, which honors the talents and gifts each brings to the whole. No matter what your talents and abilities, they are all of equal value to the whole.

Youth   I don't understand how all talents are equal. That is not my experience, it's not what I see in the world. People with more talent are paid the most.

Rabbi   Not always, but that's the way the world generally works. It's an old paradigm. It communicates that certain talents are more valuable, more worthy at the same time diminishing others by comparison. It does not honor that which underlies the talent.

Youth   What do you mean?

Rabbi   The greatest architect's talent is of no value if the structure is never built. To build it requires the efforts of the men who dig the ditches for its foundation, for without them there would be no building. Thus, the *lowest* talent is equal to the *highest* because they are mutually dependent. All talents are equal because they are all necessary to the whole. Each talent is *interdependent* so the whole can exist. Even the smallest insect is needed by nature in its particular environment. So how can we value one over the other?

Youth I never thought of it that way. What did you mean by what underlies the talent?

Rabbi We need to remember the source of life itself. The talents and abilities that you are endowed with at birth are part of your birthright. They are gifts to be developed and shared with your family, community and beyond. They are of no value if not used. Many people never fully develop their talents because they do not take responsibility for where they find themselves. They capitulate to the environment they are in and settle for less than they can become, like your former co-workers. Each talent represents an aspect of the life process that emerges through the human dimension. It is an expression of the creativity of the universe. Recall our first discussion? We are those beings through which the earth now creates new possibilities. We bring forth the second creation, so to speak.

Youth The second creation? What does that mean? I've never heard that expression.

Rabbi The evolutionary process we discussed in our first meeting, the forming of the universe and the natural environment, the emergence of the life process . . . all that is the first creation. The outcome of that creative process is the human dimension that we participate in. We are the highest expression of the first creation. The creative process of the universe now courses through our veins, expresses itself in our hopes and dreams. The structures we build, the music, art, literature, dance, poetry, dramas, customs, traditions we create are all expressions of the same creation process. They comprise the second creation. They exist only within and through the human. We are those beings through which nature's creative process now works. We represent that presence and bring into existence new possibilities on this planet. Whether that process succeeds in the long term is in our hands.

Youth So when you speak of leadership, in terms of the big picture, are you describing whose who guide and shape the second creation?

Rabbi That's a good way to put it. Leadership is a neutral process that can be orientated for good or evil. There are many examples of leaders who have led their tribes or nations to destruction. It is the result of egocentricity. The context of leadership that we are concerned with is that which *cooperates* with the underlying life process upon which we depend. The old admonition, "By their fruits ye shall know them" is a good way to recognize the orientation of any leader. The results of your present company's leadership style encourage and expand possibilities, those of your former company diminish possibilities. I'll bet their financial performance mirrors those styles as well.

Youth Yes, that's true. My present company is growing and expanding every month. Our profitability allows for growth and reinvestment. There are opportunities for everyone that will never exist for employees of my former employer.

Rabbi The second creation is just a term to describe the human dimension. It helps us identify with the process of the universe as a whole. It helps us remember who we are and what we are capable of achieving. The world you dreamed about, that fair and equitable world of universal appeal exists as a potential in creation. Leadership is required to bring it forth. Leadership is needed to give form to that vision, to encourage cooperation among others and build the common belief that it is actually possible. It will take the greatest care and faith and compassion to bring that world into reality.

Youth I think I'll start by simply learning my new role in my company and in my marriage. That's enough for now. Hopefully, that larger process will be enhanced as well.

Rabbi That's all that is asked of you. Life will bring you the experiences you need. Asking for the answer, seeing it clearly, knowing it's source and doing it . . . is the *way* of leadership.

Youth What does that mean? How does it relate to what I just said?

Rabbi Leadership involves an attitude, an approach toward problem solving. *Asking for the answer* is an attitude of expectancy, of knowing you don't know, of quiet receptivity and openness. It is the feminine principle. *Seeing it clearly* is the process of perception, of understanding our frame of reference, resolving our internal condition so we see clearly. It is both active and passive. *Knowing it's source* is acknowledging the answer comes through you, as an instrument of perception. It is not you. Finally, *doing it* is taking initiative, decision making, acting on what you see the answer to be. It's the masculine principle. The process is a movement and a rest and movement again. It is seeing, deciding and acting, then seeing again. It's a closed-loop process of discovery. Your marriage and your new position with your company are where this process of leadership is practiced. It is learned one step at a time, like any skill mastery.

Youth It sounds familiar, like issues we discussed before. The way you describe the process is different, but the theme is the same. I guess the idea of leadership is simply a way of restating the principles we have studied these past few weeks.

Rabbi Yes. We are describing in different ways principles that are universal in order to understand them better, to reveal the subtlety and practical aspects. Repetition is part of learning and internalizing what we experience.

Youth I have an appointment that I must get to. I really appreciate our conversation today. It helped diminish my nervousness about new responsibilities I will soon take on.

Rabbi Good, I'm glad it helped. I will be going on a trip after next week, so that will be the last time we meet for a while. Is there something you would like to discuss that we haven't touched on?

Youth   Yes, hope. I'd like to talk about what gives you hope for the future . . . what sustains you. ❏

Chapter

VIII.

HOPE

"The only real hope of people today . . . is a renewal of our certainty that we are rooted in Earth and, at the same time, in the cosmos. This awareness endows us with the capacity for self-transcendence . . . Transcendence as a hand reached out to those close to us, to foreigners, to the human community, to all living creatures, to nature, to the universe; transcendence as a deeply and joyously experienced need to be in harmony even with what we ourselves are not, what we do not understand, what seems distant from us in time and space, but with which we are nevertheless mysteriously linked because, together with us, all this constitutes a single world."

Vaclav Havel,
President of the Czech Republic

Chapter VIII.

HOPE

Youth   Well, we meet for the last time. I'm going to miss you and our discussions. I've learned so much, I've come so far, in such a short time. I don't know how to thank you.

Rabbi   You *are* the thanks. Nothing else is needed.

Youth   Last week we talked about leadership and the initiative it requires. As we concluded, you asked me what I would like to discuss this week, and I said *hope*. I would like to know on your journey, what has given you hope and faith in the future.

Rabbi   I thought about that during the week and what kept coming to my mind were the great cathedrals of Europe and the mosques and synagogues of the Middle East. The great structures that humans have built over time.

Youth   Why cathedrals?

Rabbi   Whenever I visit Europe or the Middle East, I spend time in these great structures, in whatever town or city I am in.

I begin to see the underlying design, the effort, work and materials used to construct it. They are magnificent. Many of these structures took over two hundred years to complete, some three hundred. Imagine four, five, even six lifetimes!

Youth I was in Rome a few years ago and visited St. Peters Basilica at the Vatican. It's hard to imagine that such a magnificent structure could even be built today.

Rabbi It couldn't. In spite of modern materials and methods, we don't have the faith or vision or patience to construct such a structure.

Youth Why not? Why do you say that?

Rabbi Our thinking, our cosmology wouldn't permit it. It must be useful, on time, on budget, easy to maintain, air conditioned, but cheap to operate . . . and more. Those considerations would never have occurred to the builders of the pyramids or the great cathedrals. It takes faith and hope to build a cathedral.

Youth Are you suggesting that we don't have that today?

Rabbi Not with our present paradigm. Think about what it took to build a great cathedral. First, you must see infinite *value* in building it; it must be *congruent* with your people's paradigm, their beliefs. The resources of an entire nation must be gathered, raw materials from far-off lands brought in and the coordinated efforts of thousands of workers and craftsmen, who will never see it completed. That requires faith. That requires hope in the future. Even the architects that conceived the design will never see it completed. Nor will the rulers, kings, magistrates, popes, or bishops who commissioned it, ever stand in its completed spaces to hear a choir sing an anthem to God. All of that required hope.

Youth   That is an eloquent example of faith and hope in the past, but how does it relate to now and our future?

Rabbi   It's the same. The magnitude of effort required to build a long-term, sustainable future will require of us the same proportionate efforts as St. Peters was to the Church of Rome.

Youth   But I don't see how you get hope from that picture?

Rabbi   Humans are capable of sustained effort over many lifetimes to achieve a common vision. That's what a cathedral teaches you.

Youth   I see.

Rabbi   We don't have a coherent vision of what a long-term, sustainable future looks like, yet. But it is emerging as we speak. We are beginning to look to the wisdom of native peoples and to those species of life that have lived on this earth far longer than humans, for guidance and inspiration. Those species and native peoples know how to live in balance and harmony with the earth, without extracting more than it can sustain. Living things have managed to turn sea and mud and rock into a life-friendly home, with smoothly undulating cycles and steady temperatures . . . without guzzling fossil fuel, polluting the planet, or mortgaging their future. These lessons are finally being appreciated and valued and modeled so that we can mimic nature's wisdom.

Youth I guess I'm not that familiar with the specifics of what you are talking about. But I can appreciate that life has managed to sustain itself for millions of years without humans so there must be lessons there, if we choose to learn.

Rabbi Exactly. *Choose* is the operative word. For generations we have viewed nature as something to conquer, to submit to our will. Now that willfulness, that human-centered paradigm, is causing irreparable harm to what sustains us all. We will learn the lessons either way . . . through catastrophic events as parts of our ecosystem shut down, or through conscious effort and decisions to live in harmony with the earth and it's community of life. The choice is ours. The outcome and responsibility is also ours.

Youth Can you give me some specifics of how we are learning those lessons? Is that where hope comes from?

Rabbi Yes. Farming is a good example. We have applied the industrial model to agriculture in order to maximize production. Our monoculture rows of wheat, corn, soybeans, citrus and other foods are utterly dependent on chemicals to resist insects, to rejuvenate the soil and to maximize growth.

These strains of modern plants are as dependent on humans as we are on them. Our methods of farming contribute to flooding and erosion. Topsoil is essentially non-renewable, yet up to six bushels of soil are washed out to sea for every bushel of corn produced. Hundreds of acres of crops are easily destroyed by hail or flood or drought because there is no diversity to limit the losses. But we are learning.

We are learning how native prairies, comprised of hundreds of species of grasses, legumes, sponges, perennials, are self-weeding, self-fertilizing, self-renewing. Huge numbers and varieties of insects also contribute to the renewal of the soil and life community. Over seventy-percent of the living mass of a prairie is underground, which soaks up heavy rains and resists damage from hail, flood or drought. Prairies have renewed themselves for millions of years without human intervention. How? We are just beginning to learn the lessons of prairie land. We are learning that incredible diversity of species is necessary for long-term survival; we are beginning to develop species of food plants that co-exist with others in a symbiotic relationship that requires vastly less chemicals, water and other resources. Even businesses in the mid-west are replacing vast lawn areas with native grasses and wild flowers that emulate the prairie, eliminating the need to water, fertilize and maintain.

Youth　That is hopeful. Are there other areas where changes like these are emerging?

Rabbi　There are many, of course. One is the energy sector of industrialized societies. It has been called the largest economic contributor to environmental degradation worldwide. Whether true or not, there's no question our production of energy is extremely inefficient and wasteful. We're consuming in one year what it took one hundred thousand years of organic growth to form. Nature, on the other hand, finds ways to harness the energy of the sun for everything. Plants, algae and some bacteria take carbon dioxide, water and sunlight and transform them into oxygen and energy-rich sugars. Then, animals like us take oxygen and those sugars and transform them back into carbon dioxide, water and energy.

Youth   So it's a closed-loop, renewable system, right?

Rabbi   Right. Plants use light energy with almost ninety-five percent efficiency which is more than four times our best man-made solar cells. What scientists all over the world are beginning to understand is how the process of photosynthesis works. As we learn how to mimic nature's way of harnessing the sun's limitless energy we will be able to transform our world. It may be possible that solar membranes will capture enough energy to power your home; molecular level structures designed to power micro-machines; molecular computers which will be thousands of times faster than the silicon chips of today; very efficient and plant-like chemical manufacturing facilities, and more. But there are problems.

Youth   What are those?

Rabbi   Our thinking, once again. Nature's way is to be very efficient on a very small scale and replicate that smallness everywhere. While we are talking, the leaves and fronds and blades of grass around us are silently assembling themselves by the trillions, to take advantage of the sun. While it may be possible to produce in the future a self-sufficient home with its own solar power, energy storage system, waste processing and more . . . our current paradigm is to have expensive, centralized, controlled distribution of these functions which fosters dependency. Our economics, our production and distribution systems, our political structures . . . all will have to change to allow nature's more efficient ways to emerge into practical reality.

Youth   That's depressing. Here we are again, on the threshold of breakthroughs that could enhance our world and the established power structure prevents it.

Rabbi   Again, you must take the long view. As we speak, hundreds of businesses are learning the lessons of a new cosmology. They are learning that flexible organizational structures are more efficient and adaptable; that more freedom and self-organization, the more overall order is created; the more stability is achieved; that collaborative, participative organizations develop a stronger sense of common effort and teamwork. They are learning new models of leadership where managers are becoming *facilitators* of change; of networking people based on interests and capability for specific tasks, then reassembling a different structure for the next task or function. Much like a tree has a structure that is flexible to withstand the winds of change.

Instead of concentrating wealth and power in a few individuals through hierarchical organizations, based on old models of reality, new organizational models are being structured to mimic nature's ways. Companies where managers and employees are the majority stockholders, engender a sense of responsibility for the whole. Some give back a percentage of their profits to the community in which they operate to honor their interdependence to that community. Some companies limit their size to maintain a human scale, sense of connectedness and responsiveness to change, yet spin off new enterprises frequently to take advantage of new market opportunities. All these are experiments in new ways of thinking about how human enterprises are designed and organized.

Youth   So are you suggesting that these changes in the way businesses and organizations are structured will facilitate and help the process of change to a better world?

Rabbi   It's part of new responses and solutions. What we are witnessing in individuals, in scientists, technicians, farmers, business people . . . are the *effects* of a new paradigm, a new way of thinking. One by one we are learning a new language, a new way of bringing nature's wisdom and experience into our lives. We are becoming the students and the earth our teacher. We are gradually learning to *value* the life system and take lessons from it.

Youth   But it's hard to see how it will change. Politics and money alone will prevent it.

Rabbi Our thinking will prevent it . . . *your* thinking will prevent it if you are not vigilant. Remember the leverage built into the change process? All change starts small, then as more people adopt a new way, a better way, others will follow. Why? Because what we have been talking about *works*. It may take many generations, it may take a millennium, but the *way of life* is the intention of creation. The only question that matters is . . . will *your* life be one of the building blocks of that new cathedral of life?

Youth That's an interesting question, because the changes in my own thinking and behavior in just a few short weeks have made a big difference in my life. For the better. I can see that if I continue along this path, my life and the life of those around me can be much better, richer, deeper than I had suspected.

Rabbi Exactly. Now that you have the tools, knowledge and insight into your own functioning, you can deal with any conflict or impasse in your life or relationships. Violence will end in you. Pass that gift to others by your example. Teach it to your children, that they may walk that same path. This is how a new world emerges.

Youth We started our talk about synagogues, mosques and cathedrals . . . what they represent to you. Can you speak more of this idea?

Rabbi You must have vision to build a cathedral. That perennial vision which has been with us since the beginning.

The capacity of the human which says, "We opt for life, we call for life". The deep longing to live in peace, to end all war forever, to stop the violence and killing, the carnage, the vengeance . . . and to heal the wounds in the human family, and the life family. To see that everything that exists is related to myself. The most profound sense of hope and possibility comes from having that perspective, that vision.

Humans are extremely sensitive, extremely aware, we are unspecialized, we are teachable and retentive. We're always questioning and always discontent, because every question leads to another riddle. We are an instrument of response, an endless capacity to perceive, and then to see more. And most important . . . we are unfinished, we're open-ended. Anything that is unfinished *can* take its next step in evolution. Courage, drive, tenacity are all resident in our genes. Because those individuals in the chain of life preceding us refused to retreat, never went back, refused to make a premature settlement for something less than humans could become.

At what price suffering and at what cost in fear and pain and disappointment was our future bought? Immense have been the casualties through those centuries. But when all seemed lost . . . the vision had almost vanished . . . up from the soul of the next generation has always come a new vision, with the will. And that great fire has never gone out. For from the deepest place inside each of us, as individuals and as groups all over this planet, we are now responding to that ancient and contemporary call . . . we opt for life. You *are* that next generation . . . in *you* resides that vision and hope.

Youth   I am reminded of a recent movie about slavery. The slave Cinque, was talking to John Adams, telling him that they were not alone, ". . . I meant my ancestors. I will call into the past. Far back to the beginning of time and beg them to come and help me. At the judgement, I will reach back and draw them into me. And they must come. For at this moment, I am the whole reason they have existed at all."

Rabbi   Native peoples are much closer to the truth about life than we. You and I are the reason *our* ancestors existed for we are as connected to them as to each other. Ancient wisdom is alive today because humans kept records and traditions and passed them from one generation to the next, never letting it go, until it reached our awareness. In the old testament tradition, which I am familiar with, God made a new covenant with mankind for a time which was to come, saying in Jeremiah, "I will set my law within them and write it on their hearts. I will be their God and they shall be my people. No longer need they teach one another to know the Lord. All of them, high and low alike, shall know me, says the Lord, for I will forgive their wrongdoing and remember their sin no more".

Youth   What does it mean?

Rabbi   It's a powerful message of the *inner changes* required of humans. The law is the way the universe operates. What works and does not work is set. What leads toward life and what leads toward death is already set. We don't have a choice. It's the issue of authority. It speaks of the right relationship with that authority, that we are the students and that deeper reality, which I call God, our mentor. We are not above the law. We each have a direct relationship to the Highest. We each have powers of perception and response to what life is asking of us each day, and in choosing the *way of life*, we heal the wounds of our past, we forgive ourselves and our neighbors, we bring love and compassion into our hearts and the world. That is how I read the message.

Youth That's a moving tribute to what I have learned from you. It's the same message. The inner capacity to deal with change and resolve my own . . . my own . . . soul. I'm beginning to have hope myself. Thanks.

Rabbi Again, you *are* the thanks. So let's get about building the new cathedral. Until we meet again, Godspeed. ❑

END